SLEEPY CHRISTIANS

How God Is Awakening A Generation
To The Present Reality Of His Kingdom

CHUCK HAGY
Foreword by Leif Hetland

**NextGen
Publishers**

SLEEPY CHRISTIANS

Copyright © 2017 by Chuck Hagy,
Foreword by Leif Hetland, Revised edition 2021

ISBN 978-1-7345229-5-2

Printed in the United States of America

Dedication

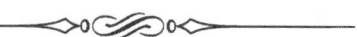

I dedicate this book to my amazing family – My wife Tara and our four beautiful girls; Abby, Emma, Ellie, and Josie. Through you, my life is filled with meaning, value and overflowing joy. With you, my days are a continual journey of exploration, discovery, and adventure. In you, I see the wonder, beauty, creativity, and love of our Heavenly Father. His supernatural Kingdom is vibrantly on display through each of your lives. I am so thankful to be your husband (Tara) and your daddy (girls). May the days ahead be filled with the continued adventure of conquering kingdoms, vanquishing evil villains, rescuing helpless victims, destroying the works of the devil, and bringing Heaven to Earth.

Contents

Foreword

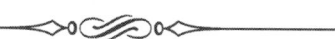

As we allow our Heavenly Bridegroom to progressively unfold His bottomless love for us, we can reach a level of intimacy where all other "desires" surprisingly lose their power to grip us. We gradually realize that all we truly yearn for is God's perpetual presence.

My Evangelical background had a worldview that "You believe, you behave, you belong." What if we first belong, and out of belonging, we believe and then out of believing what God says about us, we behave? It's not what we do that makes us who we are; it is who we are that makes us do what we do.

"Sleepy Christians" is about a person, family, church, and their story of moving from the ordinary to the extraordinary, from what is natural to what is supernatural. My experience with the author is as a Spiritual Father and friend. My joy is in seeing a family of families who no longer live as orphans, but as beloved sons and daughters of a King, belonging to a Kingdom that cannot be shaken.

My time with Chuck and his family has been a revelation of the ultimate purpose for our creation: to be with God in intimacy and to glorify Him in all we are and all we do. This family has clearly encountered God and has experienced measures of His glory. They are a family that is immersed in His love, power, goodness, grace, and strength. What they are filled with is being released to those around them.

"Sleepy Christians" is an invitation for everyone to be Born OF the Spirit, filled WITH the Spirit and walk IN the Spirit!

I was thrilled with the invitation by my spiritual son to write the forward for this book. It is personal, practical, pure, and powerful!

This book will take you higher, wider, and deeper into the Father's purpose for you so that you will also experience the transformational power of God's Love.

Leif Hetland
President, Global Mission Awareness
Author, "Seeing Through Heaven's Eyes"

Introduction

I believe one of the greatest obstacles within the Church today is spiritual sleepiness. Though we have much that captures our attention and affection, many Christians have become somewhat sleepy to God's present Kingdom. I'm not pointing fingers. I too have spent the majority of my Christian life napping while God's supernatural Kingdom advances all around me. It's not that I was fast asleep, completely unaware of God's Kingdom. It is that I had slowly, sluggishly, and sleepily drifted from my true destiny as a child of the King. My groggy condition had somewhat blurred my vision, leaving me with a fuzzy picture of God's plan to bring Heaven to Earth.

Of course, the Church has many villains. Among the chief offenders are racism, disunity, apathy, pride, greed, selfishness, competition, doctrinal error, etc. These are but symptoms of a tree that has grown roots in shallow soil. Jesus said, "No good tree bears bad fruit, nor does a bad tree bear good fruit" (Luke 6:43). We gain nothing from pointing to the bad fruit on the tree. Bad fruit only reveals that something is drastically wrong with the tree itself. Jesus promised, abundant life (now) and rivers of living water (today). Many of us have, for the most part, surrendered hope that Jesus' words carry real significance for our present lives on Earth.

Nobody prefers fake fruit over the real thing. It looks nice in the bowl sitting on the table, but have you ever picked up a fake apple, taken a huge bite, and said, "That's delicious?" I doubt you have! Perhaps the Church has become so accustomed to sleepy living that we have begun to celebrate fake fruit as if it's the real thing. We have become satisfied with comfy chairs, excellent performances, topnotch productions, and large gatherings. Maybe it's time to pause and consider what real fruit looks like within the Kingdom of God.

Not that fake fruit in itself is bad. It's only a problem when we mistake it for the real thing. In fact, the lack of holiness, power, and genuine transformation within the body of Christ has caused many outside the Church to conclude, "Perhaps the fruit's not real after all." This may also help in understanding why many from the younger generations are choosing to abandon church attendance altogether. With increasing regularity, younger individuals are concluding that Christianity, in its present form, is irrelevant to life on planet Earth.

In our journey, we are discovering that God intends life in His present Kingdom to be far more adventurous, far more transformative and far more supernatural than we imagined. We have found that when we allow our roots to grow deep into the soil of God's presence, we are awakened by a love so thoroughly satisfying, so completely nourishing, it brings forth living fruit and the abundant life Jesus promised. Deep in His love, grace is given, and faith is fostered.

Through child-like faith we enter the supernatural Kingdom of God, not only intellectually, but experientially. Abundant life can become a reality, not just when we die, but now, in this present life. We all long for the present reality of God's Kingdom, but some of us have concluded that His Kingdom is a future hope reserved for eternity. As you read, my hope is that God will awaken you to more of His presence, love and power. Further, that you will feel more and more compelled to enter the Kingdom that Jesus said is present, at hand and readily available to those who will access it through faith.

This book is written for those who suspect there is more to the Christian life than the hope of going to Heaven after we die. It is also for those who truly love God but have grown tired of the lack of transformation evident in their lives. It's for Charismatic Christians who think Evangelicals are stuffy and spiritually dead, and for Evangelical Christians who think Charismatic Christians are emotional and weird. This book is for non-Christians who view most Christians as extreme and irrelevant.

Perhaps most importantly, this book is a testimony to God's relentless pursuit of His children. It is not intended as a detailed manual on how to live the supernatural life, but is more of an invitation, from an unlikely source, to pursue more of God. If someone like me can learn to walk with God in supernatural ways, against all the odds, you can too. So, if you will, consider this book the testimony of a pastor, a family, and a church that discovered there is more of God's love and power available to His children today. It's His desire that we all discover the fullness of His present Kingdom on Earth and learn to walk in its reality.

It may seem odd that a pastor, who has served for many years in a conservative evangelical setting, would write a book about a "supernatural" journey with God, but my story is in no way unique today. God is moving around the world awakening millions to more of His love and power. He is a loving Father, relentlessly in pursuit of His children. The fact that you are about to read this book is one clue that you may be the next target of His love. Some use the term "supernatural" in a broader sense, outside of the context of Christianity, The use of the term in this book is in reference to God's ability to do the impossible whenever and however He chooses.

The intent of this book is more to describe than to convince, more to inspire than to correct. It's a gentle invitation into deep meaningful encounters with God's love. It's not intended as a means of acquiring information but of gaining encouragement and inspiration for the abundant life that Jesus promised. As you read, consider taking breaks to reflect and to be alone with God. This is intended to be an inter-actional journey with His Spirit. I pray that you keep an open heart and mind, and that you prayerfully consider your personal journey into a supernatural adventure with Him. May the process awaken in you a longing to discover, in a fresh new way, the call of Jesus to enter His Kingdom now rather than waiting until you die. It's an invitation to recapture the childlike faith of your youth and to begin dreaming with God again.

Sleepy Christians

1

Supernatural Expectation

Expect great things from God.
Attempt great things for God.

William Carey

For most of us, childhood was filled with supernatural expectation. My childhood was no different. When I received my Six Million Dollar Man doll (uh, I mean, action figure) for my birthday, I suddenly gained the supernatural ability to see with bionic eyes and run with super-human speed. When I was racing my hot wheels around the track, I suddenly became Speed Racer, winning races and catching the bad guys in their evil schemes. My life was filled with childlike fantasy. Every day began and ended with a crazy adventure. You might say each day was supernatural. Then, I grew up...

What if the supernatural life of our childhood is the normal life God intends for His children to live as adults? What if life in the Kingdom of God was intended to be one incredible supernatural adventure after another? What if, at least regarding impossible living, God never intended for us to grow up? Is it possible that when Jesus said, "Everything is possible for the one who believes," He was speaking a truth that was intended to increase the supernatural expectancy for each of God's children (Mark 9:23)?

The Games Brother's Play

Like most kids, my imagination was often captured by the wonder and magic of the holidays. I would often become carried away with thoughts of fantastic lands like the North Pole, Neverland, or Disney World. Wait! Disney World is real – right? I was always an easy target for my older brother, Darrell, who loved to fool me with his brotherly tricks. Darrell was at the top of his game on Christmas Eve since, in a young child's mind, Christmas Eve is the biggest Eve of the year.

When it was time for bed, Darrell would look out the window of our room and say something like, "Wow! Santa Claus and his reindeer just flew right over our house, look, look, there he is." I would squeeze my way past him to see out the window just as he would say, "Oh, you just missed him."

My brother would pull this stunt several times, describing how Santa and his reindeer had landed on the neighbor's roof or how Santa had just gone down the chimney of the house across the street. No matter how many times he would pull the same gag, I would fall for it every time. He loved to get me going, and it wasn't that difficult for him to fool me since I fully believed Santa was on his way to our house that same night. Looking back, I understand why my brother was able to fool me so easily. My expectation for the miraculous far outweighed any doubt or logic to the contrary. However, I have discovered that believing in something we cannot understand doesn't necessarily show that we are being foolish or gullible.

The Truth Behind Our Fantasies

Although my belief in Santa was misguided, I have come to believe in someone who has all the powers of Santa Claus and much more. I have come to trust in someone who sees me when I'm sleeping and knows when I'm awake. He can travel all over the world in one night. Not to mention that He can be in all of these places at the same time. He gives wonderful gifts to His kids, and nothing is impossible for Him. Since He has limitless power and loves to share His goodness with His kids, we too can live with a high level of supernatural expectancy in our lives.

Watching my daughter Ellie, I am often reminded of the need to remain childlike, filled with wonder and expectation. As a teenager, Ellie still exudes the same imaginative energy she had as a little girl. She has a vivid imagination that is easily activated in anticipation of holidays, birthdays or family vacations. When the weather is hot, Ellie plays Christmas music in anticipation of a cold December. She can anxiously talk about the details of her birthday in July though the actual day isn't until November. I often laugh when I look at family photos because in almost every picture Ellie looks like she was just surprised by a wonderful gift. Almost without exception, she is wide-eyed, expectant and full of joy.

I love to dream with Ellie. She keeps me young, positive and joyful. She also keeps me excited about the future with a constant expectation for impossible things. It is this same childlike expectation that enables young children to walk in God's supernatural Kingdom with relative ease. I once heard Heidi Baker say, "All children believe in miracles when they are born. It isn't until an adult teaches them miracles no longer occur that they stop believing." I agree.

Supernatural Expectation

During my late high school years, my heart became filled with anticipation for supernatural things. I had accepted Jesus as a young boy, but in high school I had rediscovered Him in a whole new light. I wanted to give my life to Him with renewed abandonment. My best friends, Brian and Perry, had also caught the "fire" for God and wanted to give themselves fully to Jesus. Much of our conversation was filled with wild dreams about our future adventures of doing crazy things for God.

We would read the Bible or listen to Christian music and discuss all the amazing things Jesus and the disciples did while He was on Earth. Our hearts were full of an expectation that God might do something crazy at any given moment. We were confident, bold and, some would say, a little crazy for Jesus; we were so alive, so passionate about God and so full of faith. We were young, naïve and, to this point, no one had told us to lower our expectation for supernatural encounters with God – at least, not yet. We also had this crazy thought that God would completely change our behavior and that sin would no longer dominate our daily lives.

Over the years that followed, I began to realize that many of the Christians who had been in church far longer than I, did not share my same level of excitement or expectation for supernatural things. I began to temper my enthusiasm until I could figure out why so many of the believers around me didn't share in my zeal. Slowly, through a good bit of teaching and logical reasoning, I concluded that the initial joy that marked my early Christian experience and expectation for a supernatural journey with God was unfounded. It was time for me to "grow up."

For me, growing up, meant divorcing myself from any childlike notion of the supernatural and grounding myself, non-experientially of course, in the unchanging Word of God. I had concluded that miracles were rare apart from brief periods of history and anyone who taught otherwise was either deceived or foolish.

2

The Gospel Is Better Than We Think

God never made a promise
that was too good to be true.
Dwight L. Moody

I remember getting a helium-filled balloon at the carnival as a child. For a little kid, few things provide hours of unaltered entertainment like a helium filled balloon. Pull it down to the ground and it pops right back up again. Bat it with your fist and it flies through the air and bounces off your sister's face. Tie a toy army guy to it and watch him fly off to outer space, or to the ceiling, whichever comes first. Then one day you wake up and find your balloon lifeless on the floor, just like every other ordinary balloon. The only thing left to do is to suck what's left of the helium from it and talk like a chipmunk. Do you feel like the Christian life is like that sometimes?

Settling for Less

Many of us accepted Jesus, expecting a life of freedom, excitement, holiness and adventure. We were like wide-eyed children, gazing out the window, waiting for God to show up and do something extraordinary. We didn't know any better. It seemed fitting that we would somehow share in the fullness of life and supernatural abundance that abides in our heavenly Father. After all, isn't that what Jesus promised to those who would follow Him – abundant life? Shouldn't we expect more from a supernatural, all-powerful God than just the promise of having victory over the devil someday after we die? I think we should! Greg Boyd highlights our dilemma in writing,

> *So, is it surprising to learn that the faith of most American Christians makes very little practical difference in their lives? In terms of what we believe, we differ significantly from non-Christians. But as it relates to how we live – what we do with our time, how we spend our money, even our basic moral practices – we differ very little. Where is the radical, trans-forming power Christians are supposed to be experiencing?*

We were created for abundant living, creative adventure, and unhindered freedom; however, many of us find ourselves just struggling to survive. I am not implying that the Christian life will be free from trials or hardship. To the contrary, Jesus clearly told us to expect persecution as His followers (Matthew 5:11). However, most of us enter our journey with Jesus expecting something supernatural to occur, both in and through us, as we walk through life with Him. However, it hasn't quite turned out the way we had hoped or expected.

Reasoning Away the Miraculous

For many of us, our initial encounter with God was somewhat supernatural. However, any hope for a continuation of this supernatural journey, is often crushed by those who tell us, "God doesn't do that anymore." And then, they clarify, "Well, it's not that God doesn't EVER do that stuff anymore; it's just that He doesn't do it as often as He did in Bible times." "He still does miraculous things, on occasion, in places like Africa or Asia where people need to see those sorts of things in order to believe; besides, we have something better–logic, reason and the unchanging Word of God."

In moments of honesty, some Christians might say something like, *The Christian life is not all I had hoped it would be. I'm thankful that I'm forgiven, but I don't see the abundant life that Jesus promised.* Sometimes the Christian life feels more like that helium balloon that has lost all of its oomph!

The Gospel, It's Better Than We Think

The New Testament word *euaggelion* means "good news." The word is a reference to the abundant life made available through the sacrifice of Jesus on the cross. The Gospel is good news because it offers transformation and freedom to anyone who surrenders their life to follow Jesus. As an Evangelical, I had always emphasized the good news concerning the forgiveness of my sin and the promise of Heaven but failed to live in the goodness of the Gospel daily. G.K. Chesterton once wrote, "The Gospel is too good to be true." I think that's why many of us only believe in part of it, the future part. From my theological perspective, the abundant life Jesus promised was mostly about a future journey to Heaven after death.

Said another way, I had always assumed that the good news of the Gospel is summarized by saying that Jesus saved me from sin and death, but I never really considered that Jesus actually paid for far more than my sin. Jesus saved me *from* sin, but He also saved me *to* an abundant supernatural lifestyle. I have discovered that the Gospel is far better news than I had once thought; it is good news for both our present and future lives.

Jesus never promised everything would be perfect in our lives once we became His followers. He never said everything would be rosy and pleasant once we give our lives to Him. He never said, "If you follow me, your kids will always obey, and your spouse will treat you with greater honor and respect; just follow me and all of your problems will vanish in thin air." However, Jesus did promise that if we follow Him, we would have "abundant life" and that "rivers of living water" would flow from within us. Concerning this reality, Dallas Willard writes,

The gospel is the good news of the presence and availability of the kingdom, now and forever, through reliance on Jesus the Anointed.

Paul writes, "For the Kingdom of God is not a matter of eating and drinking, but righteousness, peace, and joy in the Holy Spirit" (Romans 14:17). The invitation of the Gospel is an invitation to live, to a large degree, within the reality of God's eternal Kingdom now. The overwhelming joy of the Kingdom far outweighs any pleasure this world can offer; this is the good news of the Gospel and its good news for today, tomorrow and forever

The Normal Christian Life

In recent years, I have come to believe that the "normal" Christian life should be marked more by victory than defeat. Again, I am not implying that the Christian life will be easy or that we will find victory in every battle, but there is a sense that God is moving forward with His plan to bring Heaven to Earth and as His children, we are invited to participate. Living with a constant sense that God can and will do supernatural things beyond our ability to comprehend should be life as usual within the Kingdom of God. Included in the invitation to follow Jesus is also the invitation to walk in the reality of His Kingdom now.

Supernatural expectancy is the quality of the early Church Luke was describing when he wrote, "Everyone was filled with awe, and many wonders and miraculous signs were done by the Apostles" (Acts 2:43). As Jesus' followers, we should also expect a life of increasing holiness through the transforming power of God's love. I don't believe that God intends for us to live dominated by sin for the entirety of our Christian lives though many of us have settled for such a reality. What if there is the possibility to be set free from wounds that have hindered a normal, much less abundant, life in God's Kingdom. What if the brokenness of our past no longer needs to hinder us from the promises of our future?

There was a constant expectation in the early Church that God might show up and do something supernatural at any given moment. Their expectation was not misguided or foolish since their expectancy was based on their prior experience of God's activity among them. There was a constant anticipation of victory over sin, victory over brokenness, and victory over sickness and disease. In sharing our story, my hope is that you will become filled with a renewed hunger, not just for miracles or the supernatural, but for more of God's love and transforming presence. May we increasingly expect the abundant life Jesus promised His followers, and discover the righteousness, peace, and joy available through His present Kingdom.

Maybe you, like me, have found yourself in a place where you rarely expect anything supernatural from God. Maybe you have even concluded that God doesn't do miraculous things today, at least on a regular basis? Could it be that the reason we don't see the miraculous consistently in our lives is because we neither look for it nor expect it to occur? Have we settled into a life of sin and bondage that God never intended for His children? The Christian life doesn't have to be like the deflated helium balloon that sat lifeless on my bedroom floor as a child.

Maybe a lack of seeing God move in and through your life has limited your faith for the impossible lifestyle He longs for you to experience. What if today you started afresh and began asking God to reveal himself to you in new ways. What if today you started to see the Kingdom of God with clearer vision and to expect impossible things from Him. Regardless of where you are in your walk with God, there is always more of Him to know, more to love and more to experience. The Gospel is way better than we think!!

Sleepy Christians

3

Stuck In The Backyard

Ships in a harbor are safe,
but that's not what ships are built for.
John Shedd

When I was around five years old, I remember being upset with my mom because she wouldn't allow me to walk around the block with my older siblings. I could have understood her reservations in the years leading up to this point, but at five, I had matured and was one step closer to manhood, ha, ha. I deserved more freedom than I had been afforded. It wasn't fair! And I just wasn't gonna put up with it!

Was my mom unaware that I had superhuman strength and bionic capabilities, or that I had daily defended our neighborhood from the attack of evil villains? After all, I had a Batman Big Wheel for crying out loud! What dark force could come against me on a trip around the block that I hadn't encountered daily in my fight against evil? I remember standing in the backyard thinking something like, "I'll just run away from home, I'll just walk toward the edge of our backyard and keep right on walking." I wasn't sure what I would do once I left the yard, but at five years old, runaway plans aren't all that sophisticated. I spent several moments staring at the fence line before finally making my move.

Finally, working up enough nerve to "go for it," I took several steps toward the boundary that marked my independence. With each step closer to the fence line, my resolve grew stronger. Soon I would be free, no longer hampered by disrespect or the trappings of childhood. As I neared the boundary, I glanced back to take one last look at the home that I, quite possibly, would never see again. When I looked back, I noticed my mom's face staring back at me through the kitchen window—she did not look happy. Then, I heard the two words that usually meant that I was in big trouble, "Charles Henry." I knew my valiant attempt at freedom had failed.

Unfortunately, my five-year-old dreams of adventure and independence were outweighed by my fear of getting a whooping from Mama. I eventually went back to "life as usual," resigning myself, for now, to live within the confines of my own backyard. Sometimes reality really stinks! After all, what good was it to have bionic speed or the superhuman ability to leap tall buildings with a single bound if I couldn't even leave the backyard?

Facing Reality

Perhaps, subconsciously, childhood experiences like these make it easier for us to swallow the mundane Christian existence some of us settle for later on in life. By the time I graduated from seminary, my spiritual appetite for supernatural things had somewhat abated, and it was, pretty much, back to life as usual. I was right on track for the casual, highly ordinary, Christian existence that defines the walk of many Jesus followers today. Through logic and theological training, I had come to believe that the power of the Christian life was confined to the message of the Gospel. Any expectation of God intervening beyond the occasionally answered prayer was naïve.

Though I had started My Christian journey with supernatural expectations, I had "matured" in my walk with God and no longer believed that miracles or the supernatural gifts were available or necessary for believers today. I had my theological system pretty well figured out, or so I thought. I had concluded that the promise of the Gospel was primarily a promise to enter Heaven one day after I die. I also knew that obedience to the Word of God would bring about positive change in people's lives. So, my wife Tara and I decided to start a church with the hope of advancing God's Kingdom. Our primary focus was on getting people to accept and follow Jesus so they could go to Heaven one day when they died; we had little or no thought that God might want to bring Heaven to Earth through them in the present.

Our Super-Natural Plan

With a great love for God and a desire to serve Him, Tara and I began our life of ministry together. Having gained some experience in youth ministry, we planned on starting a church for those who didn't like church. Our original plan was not actually to start a church, but to start a ministry center to reach the youth of our community. By reaching young people with the Gospel, we hoped to eventually impact their parents as well.

Fresh off a three-year stint in youth ministry, we moved to a small Ohio town in hopes of fulfilling our dream of starting a radical outward-focused ministry and make an eternal impact for the Kingdom of God. We had no money, no job, no place to live and no trained team to assist us in our new endeavor. We were starting off on the wrong foot, but we were young, ambitious and naïve enough to go for it anyway.

Our goal was to tell people about Jesus and convince them to follow Him with their lives. All this was great, but it required nothing beyond our time and hard work. It was a good plan, maybe even a super plan; but it was far from supernatural.

Ministry Boot Camp

The early days, of what would later become Journey Church were more difficult than we had anticipated. Looking back, we refer to those first few years as "Boot Camp." One day I anticipate writing a book entitled, "Things Not to Do When Starting a Church." We love to tell the stories of the early years and laugh at all the silly choices and mistakes we made. I suppose the laughter is helpful in replacing the sting of failure with the joy of not having to go through the same process again.

During those early years, Tara and I poured our hearts and energy into growing the church while raising our four daughters. As parents and ministry leaders, we have always tried to make it a priority to include our children in every aspect of ministry life. We had both heard the stories of pastor's kids who had gotten bitter because they felt neglected or separate from the ministries of their parents. Each of our girls, in some capacity, has been involved with us in ministry since they were very young. We have always wanted the ministry to be a family thing and not just a mom and dad thing.

Early on, I worked full time building houses with my brother-in-law, Bill. This was a new adventure for both of us while, also, trying to figure out how to lead a group of people. I remember on several occasions, Tara and I would have long discussions wondering what we were thinking in deciding to start a church. Looking back, there are many things we would have done differently and many things we would not have done at all if we could have seen the results ahead of time. Nevertheless, many of our memories of church planting are filled with the joy of dreaming together with our family and friends about what God was going to do with our crazy ideas.

Building a Reasonable Kingdom

Over the next several years, God began to rework our thinking of church and teach us how to dream with Him rather than striving for results. Nevertheless, I proved to be a very slow learner. Though we used all the right language, saying things like, "We are doing this for Jesus and His Kingdom," there was still a big part of me that found my identity in the results. Looking back, I can see that much of my self-esteem and personal identity was dependent upon what others thought about me as a pastor, father, and husband.

Although we would open our meetings in prayer and ask God to bless our efforts, we were still very much dependent upon our strategies, planning and hard work for results. I'm aware that it's necessary to make plans and develop strategies within a church or business. Some of it worked very well for us, but our approach left us doing things backward. We would often make our plans and then move forward while asking God to bless our efforts rather than dreaming with God throughout the entire process. The problem is that natural plans lead to natural results, which isn't bad, it just falls short of the supernatural results that He desires for His children.

About seven years into the Journey, we began hitting our stride. We had bought land and a small pole barn that we renovated to suit our growing congregation. The sermons were relatively short and relevant to the concerns and needs of our people. We had a young and talented band with a crazy awesome worship leader, Les. We had also discovered the allure of fresh donuts and coffee every Sunday morning. Life Was Good.

Our building was small, but we had grown to three services. (Largely because college students love free donuts). Our staff had also grown, and we were continually strategizing about new ministry ideas and our pending building expansion plans. In many ways, we saw the fruit of what we had dreamed of when we started Journey years before. Our kingdom was growing. It was more of a reasonable kingdom than a supernatural one, but at least we were moving in the right direction, or so we thought.

Perhaps like me, you have settled for a reasonable kingdom in place of a supernatural one. Maybe you have concluded that the supernatural life is either impossible or irrelevant to life in God's Kingdom today. What we have discovered is, though we saw fruit for the Kingdom in our church, there was still more of the Kingdom available to us and to those walking with us. It turns out, God wanted to put His super on our natural. Life in the Kingdom was about to drastically change; we discovered that the Kingdom was closer and more available to each one of us than we had realized. In order to go where God wanted to take us, we needed to become dissatisfied with where we were.

Sleepy Christians

4

Dissatisfaction Guaranteed

Blessed is he who expects nothing,
For he shall never be disappointed.
Alexander Pope

Most of us have come to realize that not everything we look forward to in life turns out as we had hoped. Sometimes our expectations and reality collide leaving us dissatisfied or disillusioned. Somehow, we expect a supernatural God to bring some level of transformation and victory to our lives. When our supernatural walk with God turns out to be mostly natural with very little super, we become dissatisfied with the results. Maybe this isn't such a bad place to be in. After all, it turned out to be the one thing God used to grow our hunger and move us toward a greater pursuit of Him.

I was becoming more and more disillusioned with the whole church thing. There were a few competing thoughts that contributed to my growing dissatisfaction though I couldn't quite verbalize them at the time. At one point, a thought hit me, "So is this really what church is all about? If we do everything well, have a good band, give relevant sermons, have good donuts, offer more than the churches around us, then people will come?"

I began wondering if the success of a church was more about having a good business model and out strategizing the other churches in our area. I wondered if I was just the CEO of a Christian marketing company trying to do business better than the other churches within our consumer market. I was growing tired, almost sick, by what seemed to be a relentless spirit of competition between churches – though our church contributed to the game as much as any other.

If church was all about our strategies, why did we even need God in order to be successful? The penetrating question that kept coming to mind was, "Is it possible that we somehow planted this church without Him?" Though this wasn't true, it sure seemed true at the time.

Revolving Doors and Not So Abundant Life

Another realization I couldn't deny was the revolving door of people who would come to Journey for a season and then drop off the radar never to be seen or heard from again. We had read about this in the church planting books and had heard speakers refer to "the back door" problem in church planting conferences, but it had become a reality at Journey, and it bothered me.

I think this is a problem for many churches, both small and large alike. Sometimes it's not easy to identify, especially when more people are coming through the front door than are leaving out the back. I realize there will be turnover in every church, and some of it is necessary, even healthy, but why is it such an epidemic in the Church today? We had tried strategies to prevent this from happening – starting small groups, getting people more involved, having special classes and studies, etc. Nothing seemed to work to stop the steady flow of people leaving through the back door.

Though I was somewhat blinded to it at the time, I can now see that part of the turnover resulted from a lack of deep transformation and family connection within our people. If someone had brought this to my attention back then, I would likely have blown them off. After all, how could there be a lack of transformation? My sermons were relevant and practical, right?

The reality was that the people who came to Journey were not experiencing transformation at the level Jesus promised to those who would surrender their lives to Him. David Kinnaman highlights this problem within the American Church in writing,

Most people in America, when they are exposed to the Christian faith, are not being transformed. They take one step into the door, and the journey ends. They are not being allowed, encouraged, or equipped to love or to think like Jesus.

Part of my personal dissatisfaction with what I was experiencing in ministry came from the realization that what Jesus had promised to His followers was not fully taking place in the people of our church; not even in me, and I was the pastor. Jesus said, "I have come that they might have life and have it abundantly" (John 10:10) and "whoever believes in me, streams of living water will flow from within him" (John 7:38). As I looked at our church, and other churches I was familiar with, I didn't see evidence of the kind of radical transformation that was promised by Jesus. Either something was wrong with Jesus' words or something was wrong with us.

A Place of Grace and Love

From our early days, Journey has been a place where non-churched people felt at home. We often said things like, "This is a place of love and grace for everyone." As a result, broken people have made their way through our doors seeking help and freedom. Over the years, I have had dozens of conversations with individuals deeply in bondage who have longed to be set free. In most situations, I would listen to them, pray with them and offer some form of encouragement.

The sad truth is I rarely saw any of them set free from the deep bondage that was troubling them, not even with intense teaching or discipleship. I was somewhat angry that the devil had such a grip on their lives and, even as their pastor, was unable to get them free. These broken and wounded people would stay at Journey for a season but would eventually make their way out the back door along with countless others who had gone before them. My frustration grew.

It has been my observation that a large percentage of those who would "stick it out" in church for the longest, were those who had come from a somewhat healthy background. Those who came severely broken, with little ability to modify their behavior, would eventually fall away and stop coming. Through time we have discovered that church must become a place where regular encounters of the tangible presence of God are common or transformation will be minimal.

I believe many broken and burdened people visit church hoping to find freedom and transformation. We tend to teach them well, but our teaching rarely gives the broken an opportunity for physical, emotional and spiritual healing. Some come and remain for a season because they are filled with the hope of transformation, but over time they stop coming when they don't see a significant change in their lives. They reason, "I had thought my life would be transformed, but I am still the same person I was before I started attending church. I guess church just isn't the answer for me. I guess I will always be who I have always been."

Others jump from church to church finding little freedom or transformation regardless of which church they attend. I have come to believe that the back-door problem has less to do with small groups, church involvement, excellent sermons, great worship sets, newcomers' classes, etc. Rather, it has more to do with a lack of transformation and a general absence of true family relationships within the body of a church. What bothered me most was if Jesus had promised transformation, then I knew it was supposed to be happening for His followers, so why weren't we seeing much of it at Journey?

I once heard Bill Hybels say, "The Church of Jesus Christ is the most dynamic and life changing organization on the planet." I would often repeat these words to our congregation though I didn't fully believe them. Our mantra was, "We are all sinners in need of a Savior". This implied "Don't expect much transformation; after all, we're all just a bunch of sinners anyway."

My intention in this chapter was not to bum you out but to give you the necessary courage to move toward your supernatural destiny. God wants each of His kids to experience more of His love and power but our first step to receiving more of Him is to become dissatisfied with our current state of living with less. If you are dissatisfied with your present supernatural journey with God, take heart, there is more!

5

Why Do I Keep Falling Down?

**We must accept finite disappointment,
but never lose infinite hope.**
Martin Luther King Jr.

Growing up in Michigan, my winter weekends were often filled with trips to the slopes to go skiing with my family or friends. The beauty of fresh fallen snow and the excitement of long winding runs made up for the shortened days and bitter cold temperatures. After several years of skiing, a friend asked me if I wanted to try snow boarding instead. Since I had gotten pretty good at skiing and assumed snowboarding would be super easy to learn, I agreed to give it a try. I was wrong about the easy part!

I must have fallen down a dozen times on the first run down the mountain. Some falls were minor and insignificant, others were reminiscent of the Olympic Wild World of Sports agony of defeat commercials. Although my friend gave me tons of advice and direction throughout the day, I never went far without an epic wipeout. After hours of trying, I had mastered the faceplant, but I still stunk at snowboarding. I finally gave up and decided to stick with skiing. My entire body was in pain for days! The Christian life can be a bit like my day of snowboarding. We try and try but we can't seem to stop ourselves from falling down. Jesus promised transformation and abundant life, but many of us gave up on this promise a long time ago.

It's not uncommon for church leaders to attempt to fix the lack of transformation problem within a church by creating classes or by implementing plans for spiritual formation. For those unfamiliar with the terminology, spiritual formation describes the process of becoming more like Jesus through the practice of certain spiritual disciplines or habits such as prayer, fasting, giving, silence, Scripture reading and memorization, mission, service, etc. Developing consistent spiritual habits (disciplines) is important for our spiritual growth. However, many of us lack the motivation or discipline necessary to follow through with the process. There must be an awakening first. Let me explain.

Are the Spiritual Disciplines Enough?

Our church, like most churches, had a plan for spiritual growth, but we failed to see the results that we had expected. We discovered that the problem with spiritual disciplines is that most of us are just not all that disciplined. The truth is, most of us have good intentions but we lack the willpower to follow through consistently. Also, many of us remain trapped by the brokenness and bondage of our past. The process of spiritual formation often fails because it places the hope for transformation upon our ability to change our personal habits through disciplined behavior.

The idea goes like this: If we change our habits and consistently practice the spiritual disciplines, we will experience transformation and grow closer to God. The process of transformation begins with what we do, namely, become more disciplined in our habits. The reality is, those who struggle with the spiritual disciplines the most are usually the same ones who need them the most. Perhaps this is what Jesus meant when He said, "The spirit is willing, but the flesh is weak."

Jesus had a different approach to spiritual formation. He first sought to change the desires of His followers by bringing them into repeated encounters of the Father's love and power. His approach worked best because sanctification is primarily something we receive rather than something we achieve. I'm not saying that we don't participate. It's just that we are transformed more through His presence than through our effort, especially when we encounter Him in deeply personal ways.

When we encounter Him, our desire for more of Him increases and we are able to develop disciplined habits in our lives. When our models of transformation begin with human effort rather than God's love, the motivation and desire to change are often lacking. As Paul put it, "Christ's love compels us..." or in John's words, "We love Him because He first loved us."

The Power of Sin

We have found that spiritual transformation most often occurs through intense encounters with God's love within the context of intimate family relationships. I guess you could say that we often encounter and practice the spiritual disciplines together in family, similar to Jesus' approach with the disciples. Ironically, the disciplines become easy, even natural, when motivated by love rather than by requirement (law). We will do for love, with very little effort, what we could not do through acts of our own will. Maybe this is why, apart from deep encounters of God's love, we have neither the desire nor the discipline to foster a consistent process of spiritual formation in our lives.

We Evangelicals often assume that correct information about God will inevitably lead people out of bondage and into the abundant life Jesus promised; this is probably why the sermon has become the "holy grail" of our services. Unfortunately, the western Church has fallen behind in areas of individual holiness and transformation largely due to a lack of encounter with God's tangible presence.

The reason sin is so powerful and difficult to overcome is because sin is an experience. People aren't trapped by the idea of sin; they are trapped by the experience of it. Consider the alcoholic or the drug addict. They are not drawn to the idea or concept of these drugs; they are drawn by the encounter or the experience of them.

This explains why it is vital that our encounters with God's presence transcend our intellect and reasoning. It's no surprise that, through deep encounters with the love of God, we can be set free from the trappings that have been established through our encounters with sin. Passion is a much better thermometer than discipline when measuring the vibrancy of our walk with God. Transformation of the mind may happen through an agreement with the truth, but the transformation of the soul will only come as we experience God through intimate encounters of His love.

The Evil Twin (Religion)

The problem for many of us is that, apart from the initial encounter of salvation, we rarely experience anything supernatural in our walk with God. Having had a supernatural salvation experience, we settle into the "normal" mundane Christian life, somewhat free from regular encounters of the Lord's presence. As a result, transformation eventually levels off and we find ourselves stuck in the same sin patterns that we had been trapped in before we decided to follow Jesus.

If transformation does not continue throughout a believer's life, the fire of an intimate walk with God will eventually be replaced with its evil twin, religion. Unfortunately, transformation doesn't happen automatically and cannot be achieved through a three-step process or an intense discipleship program. The only "secret" is for each person to consistently encounter more of God's presence.

There Must Be More

Maybe you have caught yourself thinking something like, "There has to be more to the Christian life than this…." Maybe your experience of God and His Church has left you wondering what everyone is making such a big deal about. If so, you're not alone. There is a holy unrest, a growing discontent with the status quo among Kingdom believers today. It's not a new hunger unknown to generations past; it's a revived hunger which once existed in the 'Church of old' that God is awakening in those who long for and resolve to run after more of Him. God is moving among His children, awakening them to more of His love, more of His presence, and more of His power. Much like Gideon, many of us have been less reluctant to say, "where are all His miracles which our fathers told us about?"

For a growing number, deep theological discussion and eloquent speeches are no longer enough to satisfy the deep hunger we have developed for His actual presence and power. A.W. Tozer expressed the heart of those hungry for more of God by writing:

> *I want the presence of God himself, or I don't want anything at all to do with religion… I want all that God has, or I don't want any.*

When our hearts become consumed with hunger for God's presence, there are no competing pursuits in life that will satisfy. We want more of Him or nothing at all. The crazy thing about religion is that it often prevents us from truly finding God's love which, in turn, limits the level of transformation we will experience as well. Many of us find ourselves stuck in the drudgery of a religious system of do's and don'ts while God is inviting us into the joy of intimacy and romance. It's no wonder we keep falling down!

Sleepy Christians

6

Hungering For More

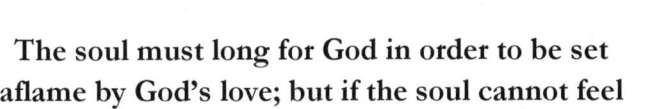

> The soul must long for God in order to be set
> aflame by God's love; but if the soul cannot feel
> this longing, then it must long for longing.
> To long for the longing is also from God.
> **Meister Eckhart**

Not long ago, I had the opportunity to go with my daughter Ellie to a father-daughter dance in our community. When the day arrived, we got all fancied up in our finest clothes, went out for a nice dinner and then headed to the dance. When we arrived, I was surprised to see that most of the fathers were standing together along the wall while their daughters went off to dance with their friends. I didn't want to be just another dad standing around with my hands in my pockets waiting for the night to end.

Now, I'm no John Travolta, but I have attended a good number of weddings in my day. Though I'm sure I looked rather foolish, I was not about to let this opportunity pass by without having a little fun dancing with my amazing daughter. I can't say she was impressed with my dancing, but I'm pretty sure she had a great time and felt loved by her dad. After the dance, a group of us went for ice cream and enjoyed the remainder of the evening out with our girls. It was a wonderful night of bonding with Ellie – one I will not forget.

I Love Romance, So What?

I'll admit, I love that kind of thing, especially when it comes with the opportunity to spend time with one of my precious girls. I'll also admit that I love romance. I used to deny it. After all, romance is for girls, right? I used to hold back the display of joy or the errant tear when the hero would risk all to save the girl, all for the sake of love. Inside, my heart would pound, but outwardly I was calm, expressionless and somewhat stoic. Maybe its age, maybe it's living with five girls, but I have somehow evolved into a hopeless romantic. Not the "Harry Met Sally" type; more of the Braveheart, Robin Hood or the fearless knight rescuing the fair maiden from the evil villain type.

I am all about heroism, bravery, chivalry, and romance. I like to think it's because God is the biggest romantic in the universe and I am becoming more and more like Him. I also like to think that it takes a real man to show emotion over the things that move the heart of God – true love, courage, sacrifice, faith, etc. Romance, the pursuit of true love, is actually at the heart of the supernatural journey and God longs for each one of His kids to pursue it daily. It is through this romance that everything in the Christian life begins to make sense and that we begin experiencing genuine transformation in our lives. Our God, without a doubt, is a divine lover. His is a love beyond understanding; immeasurably holy, perfectly selfless and absolutely pure.

I'm About To Bust

My Christian life had come full circle. I began with the expectation of a supernatural journey with God only to set aside that pursuit for the more "mature" endeavor of doctrine and theology. In reality, I was trading a romance with God and an experience of His presence for a proper, more academic journey. I believe this is the unfortunate landing pad for many devoted followers of Jesus today; this was also Jesus' big beef with the religious leaders of His day (Matthew 15:8). Somehow our tendency is to love God with our heads but keep Him a safe distance from our hearts.

Having carried the academic pursuit of knowledge to the point of frustration, my heart began to long once again for more of God himself whatever that looks like. It's not that my interest in study had ceased or that I was no longer moved by deep theological discussions about God and the world He created, it's just that I also longed for more than an intellectual journey. David Watson writes:

> The formularies and creeds of the Church, devoid of evident spiritual life, will never satisfy those who in their own different ways are searching for the living God.

After years of studying theology, my heart longed for more than just doctrinal truths about God. I wanted to experience more of Him, to know the One I had learned so much about. Henry Blackaby shares a similar thought in writing:

> You will never be satisfied just to know about God. Really knowing God only comes through experience as He reveals Himself to you. Throughout the Bible, God took the initiative to reveal Himself to people by experience.

Though I longed for more of God himself, my only fear was that my heart was deceiving me and that I was in pursuit of something that was unattainable.

Hungering for More

Though I was never extremely vocal about it, my heart had gotten to the point where something needed to change, or I would have to get out of ministry altogether. It's not that I had given up on God, but I had begun to doubt that the Church, at least our church, could ever be a place where people could find radical transformation for their lives.

I had been reading just about anything I could get my hands on that was written on revival, the presence of God, or the abundant life Jesus promised. I had spent over twenty years studying the Bible, learning theology and teaching about God, but I was sensing that there was more of God than what I had experienced to that point. A holy discontent began to grow within me as I read stories of those throughout Church history who had encountered deeper levels of God's love.

During this time, a similar discontent had been developing in my wife, Tara, as well. In desperation and from somewhat of a hunger that had begun to grow within us, we began to pray a prayer that we had discovered in a book by Bill Johnson. I had read similar prayers in the past, though Bill's prayer captured my attention. Here is the prayer as Bill relates it in his book, *Face to Face With God*,

After one such trip in 1995, I began to cry out to God day and night for about eight months. My prayer was, "God, I want more of you at any cost! I will pay any price!"

It's not that I didn't spend regular time with God before this point. I was committed to the spiritual disciplines and was faithful in my pursuit of spiritual formation. I am a pastor and, of course, pastors typically spend time with God. It was my job and obligation to pray for people. I was a "professional prayer." I had prayer lists highlighted in various colors and somewhat consistently set aside time for my "devotions." Though I believed in the power of prayer, I never really looked forward to my time alone with God because it seemed like an obligation and I couldn't see how it made a huge difference in my life.

When I spent time alone with God, I rarely felt His presence or experienced His love. Even when I did encounter Him, I never fully trusted that my experience was genuine or that it was God's presence that I was encountering. From my background, most subjective experiences are viewed with suspicion and thought to be untrustworthy. I often felt as if my prayers were bouncing off the ceiling back at me with little or no effect on Heaven. Nevertheless, I faithfully continued because I believed it was my duty as a "good pastor" to do so.

Though I had prayed similar prayers before, never had I prayed with such hunger and anticipation. Over the weeks and months that followed, that prayer, "God, I want more of you at any cost; I will pay any price," became an obsession for me. I prayed it often throughout the day, and it began to dominate my thinking. I remember at one point when I was a bit frustrated with, what I viewed as a lack of results, saying, "God, why am I not receiving what I am asking for?"

Later I realized that, in reality, my hunger for God had grown so strong that I was almost constantly aware of His presence in and around me. It was unlike any experience I ever had with God in all my years of studying and learning about Him. God had begun answering the prayer of my heart for more of Him, and everything began to change. During this season, I would find myself overcome with His presence, often in tears, wondering what was wrong with me. My craving for Him remained, and my desire for more of Him continued to grow.

Though I went about life, as usual, nothing satisfied like my time alone with Him. I had begun encountering the love of God in ways that transcended my theological understanding of Him. Though I had spent so many years serving Him, I never knew the extent of His desire to meet with me in such tangible expressions of His love. I knew that my life and ministry would never be the same again!

Sleepy Christians

7

God, The Original Hopeless Romantic

**Each time you let the love of God penetrate deeper into
your heart, you lose a bit of your anxiety,
you learn to know yourself better and long all the
more to be known by your loving God.**

Henri Nouwen

One day my daughter Josie came up to me and jokingly asked, "Hey, Dad, what's your favorite color of the alphabet, true or false?" I paused for a moment and we both started laughing. I realized there was nothing at all logical about her question. I wonder if we often approach God with a similar logic. Maybe we miss the point when it comes to our relationship with Him.

I think when we approach God from a purely academic or theological perspective, we are left with more questions than answers; we rather miss the point of what a true relationship with God is really all about. It's kinda like asking God, "What's your favorite color of the alphabet, true or false?"

Learning to be a Son

My whole perspective of God and relationship with Him changed when I made Him the primary pursuit of my affection (romance). When I pursued God above all else (at any cost), my experience of Him began to change drastically. I began to seek after God and allow myself to be open to the idea that He might reveal Himself to me beyond the usual "still small voice" I had grown accustomed to. I began to encounter tangible manifestations of His love. As odd as this seemed, my heart recognized these manifestations as expressions of God's love for me.

I had always believed in the love of God. I knew all the verses about God's love. I had taught on the love of God many times, but even as a pastor, I had never experienced His love in such intense and intimate ways. I believe I was experiencing the reality of the love that I had often taught about but rarely encountered. For the first time, I began to fully trust in His unconditional love for me which made me more capable of receiving from Him. Slowly, I began to focus on His goodness more than my badness.

Instead of coming before God spending most of our time together dwelling on how unworthy I was to be in His presence, I began to fully accept that His blood made me worthy to be with Him and to encounter His love. I had spent many years thinking that God was somehow pleased when I constantly focused on how completely unworthy I was to be His child. No wonder I was never all that excited to pray or spend time alone with God.

Somehow, I considered it a virtue to point out and dwell upon my worthlessness instead of His greatness. In His presence, I began to sense that He longed to be with me much more than I longed to be with Him. Once I fully accepted that God loves me unconditionally, just as I am, the walls of resistance that had somewhat surrounded me for many years began to fall. I discovered that He cherishes His time with His children much more than most of us realize.

Instead of praying "I'm so unworthy, I'm sure you don't want to be with me, God," I began praying prayers like, "Thank you, God, that you love me unconditionally – apart from my performance." I would say things like, "Thank you, God, that I'm your favorite and that you love me perfectly."

I don't believe that it's prideful or presumptuous for us to say that we are His favorite. We are all His favorites because He loves each of His children with a perfect and unconditional love. Though we each experience God's love differently, our theology must lead us to an encounter with Him or we will fall short of His intended purpose for our lives. A.W. Tozer put it like this:

The Bible is not an end in itself, but a means to bring men to an intimate and satisfying knowledge of God.

Identity Shift

My identity began to change through encounters of His presence. The more of His love I absorbed, the more I discovered my true identity and the less I needed to find approval elsewhere. I began to experience transformation beyond all the effects of my education. I began to sense the fullness of His peace, love, and joy. I became more peaceful, loving and joyful as His presence flowed through me.

I also gained a renewed hope for the Church and the future of the world. In a short time, I went from, "God, I don't want to do this anymore" to "God, I will go anywhere or do anything as long as you go with me." I began to feel the heart of David who said, "Do not cast me from your presence or take your Holy Spirit from me" (Psalm 51:1).

I struggled with how I would begin a conversation with Tara about the encounters I had been having with God. She would surely think I had lost my mind. To my surprise, I discovered that she had also been encountering God in similar ways during this time. When we began praying the "I want more of you at any cost" prayer, I was somewhat concerned about the cost. Would God take something from me? Would He require a huge sacrifice? Would I need to give up something of great value? However, in encountering God's presence, I became less concerned about the cost. Again, Bill Johnson writes:

Trading anything for more of God really is the greatest deal ever offered to mankind. What could I possibly have that would equal His value? I know that many say revival is costly, and it is, But when I get Him in exchange, I find it difficult to feel noble for what I've paid. Besides, revival only costs in the here and now. The absence of revival costs throughout eternity.

The abundant life Jesus promised to His followers is available for each of us today. Even more, this abundant life is intended to be the normal experience of every believer. The problem for many of us is that we have settled for a formal relationship with God when He wants a passionate love affair. The Bible, more than a theological treatise, is a love story. God presents himself as a hopeless romantic completely stricken with the presence of His lover – Us!

God, the Original Hopeless Romantic

I used to be uncomfortable with certain books of the Bible that seemed to be overly descriptive of physical love or romance. I couldn't quite understand how a book like Song of Solomon made it into the Canon of Scripture. That was before I became a victim of God's relentless and powerful love. Now, my heart is moved by verses like, "I am my beloved's, and my beloved is mine" (Song 6:3) or "How much more pleasing is your love than wine" (Song 4:10).

The first question of the Westminster Catechism asks, "What is the chief end of man?" The answer is "To glorify God and enjoy Him forever." Evangelicals typically relate well to the first part of the answer but poorly to the second. Enjoying God seems a bit too touchy-feely for most of us.

However, nothing quite compares to the encounter of God's relentless love. Nothing can take its place, not doctrinal truths, not theological understanding, not even our ministry to others. I have come to believe, more than any other defining characteristic, its divine romance between God and His children that most accurately describes the nature and purpose of the Kingdom. John Eldredge eloquently writes:

> *The story that is the Sacred Romance begins not with God above, the Author at his desk, but with God in relationship, intimately beyond our wildest imagination, heroic intimacy. The Trinity is the center of the universe; perfect relationship is the heart of all reality...we long for relationship because we were made in the image of perfect intimacy.*

It's the pursuit of intimacy with God that is essential and central to the abundant Christian life that Jesus promised. Without it, our transformation will be limited and God's desire to work through us in supernatural ways will be hindered. When we connect with Him on a deeper level, He will awaken dreams within us and move us toward our supernatural destiny.

Sleepy Christians

8

If You Can Dream It, You Can Do It

It's kind of fun to do the impossible;
If you can dream it, you can do it.
Walt Disney

A few years back, I walked into my youngest daughter, Josie's, room to tell her something when I heard a conversation taking place inside. As I opened her door and glanced in, I realized she was caught up in her own fantasy world, fully unaware that I had entered her room. I back-pedaled and closed the door just enough so I could see her, but she couldn't see me.

I watched as she had an in-depth conversation with her imaginary guests. I am amazed at Josie's ability to create an entirely parallel reality with little or no effort. Her capability to interact with her imagination with relative ease is a wonderful reminder of a child's ability to dream and create. I believe this quality in children is something God wants us to recapture in our adult lives. I am not referring to believing in fantasies or make believe, but in becoming open to a reality that is beyond the grasp of our five senses.

One of the great things about being a parent is that we get to watch the wonder and fantasy that naturally exists in our children. It is quite astonishing that they can dream so easily beyond the physical realm. The crazy thing about this encounter with Josie is that it never occurred to me to rush into her room and point out how illogical she was being.

I didn't think to sit her down and have a conversation with her about the silliness of her fantasy and imagination.

There is something very powerful about Josie's ability to use her imagination to dream up impossible adventures and unseen worlds. As I grow older, I hope I become more and more like her in this way. This is also the quality in her that I most hope she can maintain as she grows older, because the supernatural life requires a wild imagination and a willingness to dream with God.

If You Can Dream It, You Can Do It

Why are we humans so moved by wonder and fantasy? Why are we drawn into stories that capture our imaginations and take our minds on magical adventures? One day, on a family trip to Disney World, we came across a quote by Walt Disney that said, "If you can dream it, you can do it." I'm not sure if he was fully aware of it or not, but I think Disney had captured a truth that has existed in the hearts of boys and girls, men and women since creation; a truth that God invites us to enter into daily.

God created us with the ability to dream and imagine, so there must be some truth to Walt Disney's words. Jesus affirmed the extent of God's creative ability when He said, "With God all things are possible" (Matthew 19:26). Amazingly, Jesus didn't stop with God's creative ability, but included us by saying, "Everything is possible for one who believes" (Mark 9:23). Could this be true? Was Jesus exaggerating for dramatic effect? I don't think so. I believe Jesus was presenting a vital truth that few of His followers take seriously today. I love it when Jesus says crazy things like this, especially when He includes us in His statements.

It's no coincidence that, even as adults, our hearts are drawn to fantastic tales of wild adventure. Are there greater truths behind the stories and fantasies that capture our imaginations and cause our hearts to soar with childlike wonder? I believe there are! Allowing our children to discover reality without stifling the fantasy and mystery of their imaginations is a huge part of their growth and development, both in logic and spiritual discernment.

During our annual trek to Disney World, I love to see the smiles on each of our girls as they watch the princesses. Their eyes light up when they see Cinderella, Belle or one of the Disney princesses all fancied up in their beautiful dresses. Though they have grown older, there is still a little girl within each of them who knows that they are still princesses in God's supernatural Kingdom.

When we allow our children to dream and discover without continually questioning the validity of their dreams or fantasies, we are not necessarily affirming their belief in the fantasy itself, but in the greater truths the fantasy represents. Is it possible that much of what we dream about is actually pointing to greater truths about God and the universe He created? Absolutely!

Imagine That!

A major shift in thinking has occurred within the Church since Jesus' day in regard to the mind and the imagination. In Jesus' world, the imagination and intuition were considered valuable and necessary compliments to human reasoning. Within modern thought, the words "imagination" and "imaginary" have become somewhat synonymous. It would have been unthinkable to the Eastern mind to separate the intellectual learning process from the revelation received through intuition and imagination.

The western world has little value for the imagination due to the influence of rationalism, an over-emphasis on reason and the impact of Greek philosophy on some prominent, early Christian theologians. By over-emphasizing human logic and discrediting the imagination, many believers have become crippled by a theology that rejects the supernatural life God has intended for them.

Throughout Scripture, God expected His people to use logic and reasoning to discern, problem-solve and make rational decisions. However, He also expected them to use their imaginations coupled with faith to experience the impossible. Jesus said:

> *I tell you the truth; the Son can do nothing by himself; he can do only what he sees his Father doing, because whatever the Father does the Son also does.*
> *John 5:19*

How did Jesus see what the Father was doing? I believe the Father used Jesus' imagination to reveal truth and give direction. The New Testament gives us every reason to believe that Jesus intended His followers to use their imaginations in a similar way to encounter the miraculous in their daily lives. There is a very common saying, "I will believe it when I see it." In the Kingdom, the principle seems to be, "You will see it when you believe it."

There is something about childlike faith, empowered by the imagination, which brings the realities of Heaven into the physical realm of Earth. I believe this is why Jesus was constantly telling stories. He knew that if He could teach His disciples to use their imaginations, they would begin to encounter more of the supernatural nature of the Kingdom.

One day last year, I was leaving a meeting with a fellow pastor when God used the canvas of my imagination in a powerful way. As I was pulling out of the parking lot, I saw a picture flash in my mind of a man with a cane limping into one of our local restaurants. I was heading to that restaurant to pick up lunch for the girls so I said in my heart, "God if I see this man when I arrive at the restaurant, I will ask him if I can pray for him." As I approached the restaurant, I saw, in the physical, the very picture that God had painted on my imagination; a man with a cane entering the restaurant as his wife held the door for him. I said something like, "Here we go again God; You are so crazy."

When I approached the man and his wife inside the restaurant and asked if I could pray for him, he was very receptive to my offer. God led me to pray for his leg, but also for his heart. As I prayed, God directed me to pray for the difficult time that their family was going through. I prayed that God would bring peace and comfort to his family and that they would experience God's love during this time. I also prayed that God would heal the hurt and pain within his heart.

After the prayer, the man and his wife were in tears. I said, "Thank you for allowing me to pray for you." As I began to walk away, they stopped me and said, "You have no idea what your prayer means to us, our family is going through a very difficult time." I said something like, "I'm not sure what you are going through, but God does. He really loves you and cares about your pain. He cares so much that He showed me a picture of you several minutes before I arrived here." Moments like these remind us of God's desire to use our imagination to bring Heaven to Earth. Like Jesus, we do what we see our Father doing.

Sleepy Christians

9

Dreaming Like A Child Again

In almost everything that touches our everyday life on
planet Earth, God is pleased when we're pleased.
He wills that we be as free as birds to soar and sing
our maker's praise without anxiety.

A.W. Tozer

Once on a family vacation to Florida, we stopped at a restaurant for dinner. Often, as we are finishing our meal, we stop and ask God what He might want to share with our waitress or waiter. On this occasion God immediately gave our daughter Josie the word "nurse." Josie then said something like, "I think she wants to be a nurse." God then gave each of us words or pictures that supported the word that Josie heard.

When it was time to pay the bill, we shared our words with the waitress, emphasizing that God sees her as a very loving person who enjoys caring for others. We shared that perhaps she might consider a career in nursing. Tears filled her eyes and then she confirmed that she had wanted to pursue a career in nursing but wasn't sure if this was the right direction for her life.

She shared that she had just asked God to confirm if this desire was in line with His plan for her life; God used our words to give her the confirmation she wanted. When we take moments from our day to stop and ask God to paint pictures on our imaginations or to enable us to hear His voice, He may use us in supernatural ways to change someone's life.

Imagination and Freedom

When Jesus said, "Anyone who will not receive the Kingdom of God like a little child will never enter into it" (Luke 18:18), maybe He wasn't being critical, but simply stating reality. It takes childlike faith (wonder) and expectation to experience the Kingdom of Heaven on Earth. It's impossible to experience the Kingdom through reason alone because miracles by their very nature transcend human understanding. Perhaps this is what Jesus meant when He said, "If you believe (like a child), you will see the glory of God" (John 11:40). Using the imagination is essential to life in God's Kingdom. Following Jesus will be virtually impossible without it.

Much of the freedom that is available through our supernatural walk with Jesus will come as we allow God to renew our minds. God has created us with a tremendous ability to encounter Him. Later in this book, we will discuss, in greater detail, how God brings freedom from brokenness and past wounds as we encounter Him through our memory and imagination.

Universal Truths of God's Invisible Kingdom

Have you ever thought that maybe our children, in all their wild daydreaming, may be more in touch with the reality of God's universe than we are as adults? Maybe children are more firmly grounded in God's created reality because they are not as far removed from God's presence when He crafted them within the womb (Psalm 139:13).

Is it possible that, as adults, time has slowly lulled us into a slumbering state of forgetfulness where we have lost contact with the dreams and creative power we were connected to as children? What if we have drifted from reality because we have failed to offer our imaginations as a canvas for God to speak to us and have limited our dreams to thoughts or concepts we can rationally comprehend or explain?

It's as if there is a story God has woven into the workings of the universe that children automatically accept without the need to explain or rationally understand. Have you noticed that the themes we once loved as children haven't changed much now that we are adults? We love action, suspense, and excitement. We love the same grown up version of chivalry, fantasy, and adventure that we loved when we were children. We love them, that is, if the storyline matches the reality of God's created order.

Why is it that every good book or movie has certain characteristics that make it good? From my perspective, there are always good guys and bad guys, but the good guys have to win or the movie stinks. There are heroes and villains in most every story, but unless the heroes emerge victorious in the end, we leave confused and frustrated. Isn't it true, unless the brave knight rescues the fair maiden and rides off into the sunset, we are left with an unsettling feeling and sense of injustice? It's never okay for the evil villain to escape with the fair maiden while the hero is left to face certain death. Good must win, evil must be defeated. The story of God's good universe demands it to be so.

Why do we have such a hard time with injustice? Why do we get all bent out of shape when things aren't made right or when fairness doesn't prevail? Have you noticed that children never need to be taught to cheer for the good guys? I'll bet you've never had to explain to your son or daughter what justice looks like in the real world. They know when they are being treated unjustly. If you don't think so, try cheating them out of the bigger piece of cake or the front seat of the minivan. I think it's because each child is born with an innate sense of justice.

Is God Boring?

Children are born with an understanding of the "way things are supposed to be." God has written certain universal laws into the hearts of those who were created in His image. Everything in the universe is created to point to a good and joyful creator. Both adults and children are drawn to the impossible realities of God's amazing universe. We are all moved by the same universal symbols of good: love, sacrifice, chivalry, courage and supernatural adventure. The only difference is children fully believe that nothing is impossible and that all of these characteristics still fully exist within the realm of God's eternal Kingdom. Children maintain the ability to see heavenly realities and dream with God.

Recent studies show that younger generations are leaving the Church and abandoning their faith more than any time in recent history. Though there are a number of contributing factors, many young people are saying that they have tried the Christian faith and found it unfulfilling, irrelevant, and boring. Chuck Coulson comments by writing:

Christianity is the most exciting story ever told. It needs to be told, not the way we typically dumb it down, but the way it is. Unfortunately, I believe young people have a legitimate gripe when they say it is boring – that's the watered-down version of Christianity that they have experienced. This is something we must overcome.

Is it possible that the reason an increasing number of young people are finding the Christian life boring is that we have been stifling their dreams and discouraging them from using their imaginations to encounter heavenly realities? I believe that it's God's desire for each of His children to dream with Him and to allow Him to use their imaginations as a means of inviting them into the impossible adventures of His present Kingdom. Anything less would be, well...boring.

Seeing and Doing

Awhile back, several groups from our church went out into our community on "treasure hunts." On this treasure hunt, we were not looking for material treasure, but for people with whom we could share God's love. Before we left the church, we asked God to paint pictures or words in our minds so we could find the "treasure" (people).

In actuality, we were asking God to use our imaginations as His canvas to communicate His heart with us. We asked God several questions as we prepared for our journey. First, we asked Him where He wanted us to go. Then we asked Him for a description of the person or persons we would meet there. We also asked Him what these people were going through or were in need of in their lives. Finally, we asked God for details that might help us in our search. Here are some of the items that we wrote on our list based on the pictures or words God placed in our minds:

Dairy Queen	girl with red hair	Red Rose
2 Girl Names	"She misses her dad"	Hurt ankle
Boy name	Striped shirt	

Our group got together; compared clues, and determined that God wanted us to go to Dairy Queen for our treasure hunt. So, we packed into the mini-van and headed to DQ.

As we pulled into DQ, we saw a mother and her teen children walking to their car. One of the teen girls had dyed her hair a bright red color. We parked the van and ran over to this family. Holding our treasure maps, we said to the family, "We are on a treasure hunt, and we believe you are the treasure." They all looked at us as if we were from another planet. We explained what we were doing and began to show them our clues. We mentioned a name that God had given us and one of the girls said, "That's my name."

We looked at our clues again, and then I looked at the girl with red hair and said something like, "God said you are hurting and that you really miss your dad." Tears began to well up in her eyes and the eyes of her mom. Her dad had recently passed away. We looked at our clues once again and saw that God had given us the words "red rose." When she saw this clue on our paper, she showed us the tattoo of the red rose she had gotten when her dad passed away. By this time, we were all greatly moved by the love that God was pouring out onto this family.

Looking once again at our clue list, we saw that we had also written the words "boy with a striped shirt" and "an ankle or knee injury." At that point, we realized there was a teen boy sitting in the front of the car. The boy was wearing a striped shirt and had just recently been in a skate-boarding accident. He had badly injured his ankle and knee and had been to the doctor that same day for treatment. We asked him if we could pray for God to heal him, and he said, "Yes."

After praying for him, the boy got out of the car to check his leg. He moved it slowly, and then a big smile came across his face. The pain had left his ankle and knee! We all gathered around this family and prayed over them, asking God to shower them with His love. By the end of our short time together, we were all amazed at how God had used the canvas of our imaginations to speak words of life and bring transformation to this amazing family.

Maybe it's been a long time since you've dreamed of doing anything "unreasonable" or impossible. Maybe you, like me, have limited your Christian life to dreams that are logical and somewhat reasonable. Maybe you have come to view the imagination as a childish aspect of youth, irrelevant to the "grown up" Christian experience. Could it be that your lack of encounter with the supernatural impossibilities of the Kingdom coincides with your reluctance to dream with God, allowing Him to use your imagination as His canvas to paint truths that are too extraordinary for your rational mind to comprehend?

Many of us have settled into a journey with God that is anything but supernatural. If you listen, it's possible that you will hear God tenderly inviting you to return to the faith of your childhood; to awaken to the impossible adventures He has placed within you, to dream like a child again.

10

Childlike Faith

**Someday you will be old enough
to start reading fairy tales again.**

C.S. Lewis

Our family takes a trip to Disney World every winter. It's been an
education over the years in stretching our collective, creative, and
imaginative energy. I remember our first trip to Disney when our oldest
daughter was three years old. We had decided to visit the Magic
Kingdom because we thought Abby would enjoy the wonder and
fantasy of the Disney characters and the Cinderella castle. I wasn't
expecting there would be much at the Magic Kingdom that would be of
interest to "mature" adults like me. But, of course, I was wrong.

It didn't take long before I was caught up in the fantasy of this
wonderful place "where dreams come true." Somehow, I found myself
captured by the wonder and magic along with all the other children,
young and old alike. There is something about the wonder of this make-
believe kingdom that somehow mimics the reality of God's eternal
Kingdom.

I knew it was time to come home when I got a little misty-eyed
during the coronation ceremony for Cinderella and Prince Charming –
enough is enough. Still, we have returned to this dreamy place many
times since that day.

The Faith of a Child

The wonder of childhood is somehow attached to a child's ability to believe in and dream about things they can't see. When Jesus said we must have the "faith of a child," is it possible He was saying a lot more than "you really need to trust God?" Although I do believe Jesus wants us to trust God, I believe He was talking about trusting God in such a way that we expect the miraculous to take place consistently in our lives. Jesus continually challenged his disciples to live with the kind of faith that expects the impossible to occur at any moment.

One of the most vivid pictures in the New Testament is when Jesus calls a little child to stand next to Him and says, "I tell you the truth unless you change and become like little children, you will never enter the Kingdom of Heaven" (Matt 18:2). When little children were brought to Jesus for prayer, the disciples rebuked those who brought them. When Jesus saw this, He said, "Let the little children come to me, and do not hinder them, for the Kingdom of Heaven belongs to such as these" (Matt 19:14).

Though it is difficult to be certain of everything Jesus meant in these passages, there are a couple of truths that seem clear from Jesus' words. First, children are qualified to represent the Kingdom of God because of some childlike quality they possess. Second, Jesus wants adults to become increasingly like the children they once were. Somewhere wrapped up in this concept of childlike faith we discover the secret of God's eternal Kingdom. Jesus wants His followers to have childlike faith, but what does childlike faith look like?

I have always loved to watch the extreme optimism and creativity that naturally exists in children from the time of birth. I thoroughly enjoyed those moments when our children were very young. I observed them as they were completely taken away with their imaginations and watched while they twirled around in their dresses as beautiful princesses. I cheered them on when they defeated evil villains with their magical plastic wands and celebrated their prominence when they ruled over vast kingdoms as good and fair queens.

If you have children of your own, I'll bet you know what I am talking about here. Maybe your son tied a towel around his neck, spread out his arms, and jumped off the couch, fully believing that he was flying, at least for a moment. We have all been entertained, if not amazed, by the relentless imagination and wonder of the young children in our lives. It's as if God puts something in children that causes them to believe they're invincible, that they are fighting for justice in the universe, and that nothing is impossible for them.

Peter's Childlike Faith

One of my favorite stories in the Bible is the story of Peter asking Jesus to call him out onto the water. It would have required a good bit of childlike faith to ask, as Peter did, for Jesus' permission to come out of the boat onto the water. He said, "Lord if it is you, tell me to come to you on the water" (Matt 14:28). I think what made Jesus so excited about Peter's request was that Peter had the kind of faith necessary to believe for something that was illogical and seemingly impossible.

As a result of his request, Peter was invited out of the ordinary and mundane, and into the extraordinary and supernatural. Jesus simply said, "Come," and in a moment, Peter found himself defying the laws of gravity and all logic as he walked on the water toward Jesus. Can you imagine the amazement and wonder of the disciples, still in the boat, as they watched Peter do the impossible? We are not told how long Peter walked on the water before he was distracted by the wind and waves. But, at some point, he became fearful and began to sink. Jesus reached out His hand, saved Peter, and said, "Why did you doubt?"

I don't think Jesus used a scolding or disappointing tone when he said this. I believe Jesus was thrilled with Peter's accomplishment and was conveying something like, "Peter you were starting to believe like a child again; you were walking on water; why did you stop believing?" One could argue that the disciples, still in the boat, also had faith in God. I'm sure at some level this is true; however, at this moment, Peter had the kind of faith that believed God for the impossible, and as a result, was able to participate in (enter into) the Kingdom of God on Earth.

Faith is Spelled RISK

Just like Peter getting out of the boat, the journey into the impossible requires childlike risk that transcends logic. My daughter Emma has taught me a lot about risk. As a young girl, she loved to go to the nursing homes and pray for the senior citizens.

I remember a time when we were out shopping for school clothes when I noticed a young man with an ankle brace. Since I wasn't feeling particularly risky that day, I tried to distract Emma from seeing the young man. From experience, I knew if Emma saw him, she would say something like, "Dad, there's a guy with an ankle brace; let's go pray for him." She is a faith in action kind of girl.

Of course, Emma spotted him, and a few minutes later we were praying for him right there in the middle of Old Navy. I have decided if Emma can step out and take risks, there is no reason I can't do the same from time to time as well. Since faith comes from the heart, not the head, the Holy Spirit will inspire a daring boldness, enabling us to follow our hearts into impossible situations.

I realize that not all risk looks like praying for a complete stranger in public. God will move each of us to step out of the boat in different ways. The supernatural life is not limited to extroverts, though it does require a level of risk. In pursuing God as a family, we took many trips and traveled hundreds of miles to position ourselves to hear from God. We began to get out of our comfort zones all for the chance of catching more of His presence.

There will be moments in your supernatural journey with God when he calls you out of the boat into the uncertainty of the wind and waves. Often, the quickest way to encounter God is to jump in and take a few risks. I heard someone once say, "I knew someone who grabbed a cat by the tail and learned ten times more about cats than if he hadn't." I never dreamed that I could come up with a legitimate illustration using cats. Sorry cat lovers.

Another great training moment in the life of the disciples came when they were in a boat with Jesus, and a great storm arose on the lake threatening to capsize the boat. The story goes like this:

One day Jesus said to His disciples, "Let us go over to the other side of the lake." So, they got into a boat and set out. As they sailed, he fell asleep.

A squall came down on the lake so that the boat was being swamped, and they were in great danger. The disciples went and woke him, saying, "Master, Master, we're going to drown!" He got up and rebuked the wind and the raging waters; the storm subsided, and all was calm. "Where is your faith?" he asked his disciples. In fear and amazement, they asked one another, "Who is this? He commands even the winds and the water, and they obey him."

Luke 8:22-25

The crazy thing about this story is that Jesus was asleep in the boat while all this turmoil was taking place. Some might suggest that Jesus was pretending to be asleep just to see how the disciples would respond. I don't think Jesus was faking or else the Bible would specify. The disciples woke Jesus up and said, "Master, Master, we're going to drown!" Jesus replied, "Where is your faith?"

The Logical Side of Faith

Although it seems clear that Jesus was frustrated with the disciples in this passage, I don't think He was frustrated because they interrupted his nap or because they were afraid of the storm. I think Jesus was frustrated because, after all they had seen and heard, they still did not believe like children. Their faith for the miraculous was almost unaffected by their many encounters with God's power.

Could it be that Jesus fully expected his disciples to speak up and calm the storm on their own? I think so. Perhaps Jesus was saying something like, "Where is your faith? Haven't you seen and experienced enough of the Kingdom of God to cause you to believe like children again? Shouldn't you be able to handle this storm on your own by now?" When God reveals a reality to our minds that transcends our comprehension, it no longer remains logical to act within the confines of our prior understanding.

Before we put this topic of childlike faith to rest, let's look at one more passage concerning Jesus' expectation of childlike faith among His followers. In Matthew chapter 16, Jesus is once again in a boat with His disciples when a discussion, maybe even an argument, develops between the disciples over their failure to bring bread along with them on the trip. The discussion begins like this...

> *When they went across the lake, the disciples forgot to take bread. "Be careful," Jesus said to them. "Be on your guard against the yeast of the Pharisees and Sadducees." They discussed this among themselves and said, "It is because we didn't bring any bread."*　　　　　*Luke 16:5-6*

It seems that one of them had forgotten to bring food along and they had interpreted Jesus' statement as a reprimand for their forgetfulness. The discussion is quite ironic since it occurred on the heels of Jesus' miracle of multiplying bread and fish. Jesus then interrupts their conversation...

> *Aware of their discussion, Jesus asked, "You of little faith, why are you talking among yourselves about having no bread? Do you still not understand? Don't you remember the five loaves for the five thousand, and how many basketfuls you gathered? Or the seven loaves for the four thousand, and how many basketfuls you gathered? How is it you don't understand that I was not talking to you about bread? But be on your guard against the yeast of the Pharisees and Sadducees." Then they understood that he was not telling them to guard against the yeast used in bread, but against the teaching of the Pharisees and Sadducees.*　　　　　*Matthew 16:7-12*

Once again, it is clear that Jesus was frustrated with the lack of faith displayed by the disciples. His frustration was justified because the disciples had completely limited their faith to human reason, even after they had been involved with the miracles of food multiplication.

After listening long enough to their endless squabble, Jesus stops them and asks, "Why are you talking among yourselves about having no bread? Do you still not understand?" (Matt 16:8-9) I think Jesus is saying something like: "Why do you still have concerns about bread when you have already seen bread multiply, by your own hands, on two other occasions? Shouldn't you have childlike faith in the area of food multiplication by now?"

Jesus wasn't frustrated because they forgot the bread; he was frustrated because they had seen the Kingdom of God come in power, yet they were still unable to believe in what they did not understand. Logic had become a stumbling block to their childlike faith. They were still thinking like adults when they should have been thinking like little children again. Though Jesus could have fed the multitudes himself, He instead turned to His disciples and said, "You feed them." Jesus fully expects His followers to possess the kind of childlike faith that brings Heaven to Earth and sees the impossible as a daily part of the normal Christian life.

For some, the Christian life has been limited by the kind of faith that resembles that of the disciples who sat in the boat while Peter walked on the water toward Jesus. It's not that our faith is less valid or real, it's just that it often falls short of the supernatural lifestyle God desires for His children because it is neither radical nor childlike. The supernatural journey begins with childlike faith. Childlike faith includes trusting God for both the mundane and the extraordinary, for the routine and the miraculous, for the simple things of life, as well as the impossible adventures that await us in God's present Kingdom.

Sleepy Christians

11

Jesus, Football & A Green Beret

**To one who has faith, no explanation is necessary.
To one without faith, no explanation is possible.**

Thomas Aquinas

When I was in junior high school, I had a lot of fun playing pick-up football games with the other kids in our neighborhood. Typically, my team would win in dominating fashion. I'd like to say that our victories were 100% due to my athletic prowess, but it might have had a little to do with my brother in law Billy, the 6 foot 3 ex-green beret who I always brought with me to the games.

Not only was Billy ten years older and a hundred pounds heavier than any kid in our neighborhood, he was also in peak physical condition. As a result, "we" dominated each game. The neighbor kids usually went home beaten and battered while I basked in "our" victories. Childlike faith requires that we learn to partner with Jesus in bringing Heaven to Earth. When we partner with Jesus, it's kind of like having a green beret on your junior high football team.

Childlike faith is an essential starting point to our supernatural journey with God. Without it, it will be difficult to see the realities of heaven come into the earthly realm. It's not that God is saying no or is withholding the supernatural realm from us, but faith (trust) is a prerequisite to life in the Kingdom of God. Maybe this is why the author of Hebrews writes:

And without faith, it's impossible to please God because anyone who comes to Him must believe that He exists and that He rewards those who earnestly seek Him.   *Hebrews 11:6*

This passage is often misunderstood and presented as a statement of God's disappointment with those who fail to trust Him. Rather, it is more of a description of how God takes great pleasure in the faith-filled achievements of His children. Our Heavenly Father takes no pleasure in our failures or in our inability to trust Him for great things. Instead, He rejoices in our accomplishments and finds great pleasure in our victories won by faith, like any good Father would.

Abundant Kingdom living is accomplished through childlike faith; therefore, it makes sense that God takes no pleasure in our faithlessness. He sees all that we can be and expects far greater things for each of His children. By acting in faith, we begin to see a breakthrough in our lives while also bringing great joy and pleasure to our Heavenly Father. I believe this is what James meant when he said, "Faith by itself, if it is not accompanied by action, is dead" (James 2:17).

The Faith of Jesus

This is not a challenge to strive to work harder at mustering up faith in our minds as if faith is somehow the byproduct of our diligent effort. We cannot conjure up faith by concentrating or thinking harder about everything we should believe. Faith is the fruit that springs up within the heart of those who dwell (remain) in His presence; it is actually the faith of Jesus that we receive through intimacy that moves mountains, not our own faith. (Ephesians 2:8; Galatians 2:20)

As we grow in intimacy with Him, we come to trust Him more completely. The more we know Him, the more we trust Him like little children. Faith is a relational byproduct of being with Jesus (Acts 4:13). It is often assumed that faith is somehow conjured up within the mind; however, true faith arises from a heart that has been feasting on God's love and has learned to trust Him. The faith of Jesus is imparted to us through intimacy, it is not an intellectual choice as we often assume.

True faith will always move us to action; this is not limited to evangelism or living moral Christian lives, but to every area of our journey with God. Unlike the English word for "faith," the Greek word *pistis* transcends mental ascent to include action. The New Testament use of "faith" is not limited to our thoughts, but rather describes the action that arises from our hearts. Faith is an action word; this is why James says, "I will show you my faith by what I do" (James 2:18).

The Kingdom – It's Closer than You Think

So, when Jesus said, "Unless you change and become like little children, you will never enter the Kingdom of Heaven," He was not speaking judgment, but hope. Jesus was not condemning us for our lack of faith; He was challenging us to have faith of another kind, the kind we used to have when we were little children. Some have supposed Jesus was talking about a future Kingdom (Heaven) in this passage. They suppose Jesus is saying something like, "If you don't become like little children, you cannot go to Heaven when you die." However, Jesus wasn't speaking of entering a future Kingdom but a present one.

The modern mindset has made the word "Kingdom" synonymous with "Heaven." This idea is far from Jesus' thinking since His use of "Kingdom" in the New Testament was most often in reference to the present reign of God extending into the future. This is why Jesus said that the Kingdom of Heaven had "come near" or was "at hand" (Matt 4:17). Jesus was saying that if we return to the kind of faith that we had as small children, when we believed nothing was impossible, we will begin to see the Kingdom of God manifest in and through our lives. Childlike faith makes the present Kingdom available to each of us. Without it, it will be impossible for us to see or to enter into His present Kingdom on Earth.

Accessing the Kingdom

One day at a conference in Kentucky, I was "elected" to pray for a woman sitting in front of me who had stood up for prayer. I asked her what I could pray for, and she said she had been in a car accident 12 years earlier which left her with severe damage to her back and legs. She said she was in constant pain and had minimal feeling in her legs and almost no feeling in her feet. I wasn't accustomed to expecting much through my prayers, but I thought, "Oh, well, it can't hurt to pray." Though I was shaking with fear, I knew that Jesus was inviting me to step out of the boat.

When I put my hand on the woman's back and began to ask Jesus to heal her, she said she felt an intense heat in her back and hips; no one could have been more surprised than I was in that moment. Some have come to associate heat or electrical sensation with the body's response to God's healing power. As I continued to pray, she became overcome with God's presence and could no longer hold herself upright. She fell back into her chair and rested; I wasn't sure what to make of the whole thing. Afterward, the woman shared that all the pain had left her back and that she had gained some feeling back in her legs. We celebrated and thanked God for all He was doing in her life.

The following morning when I saw her coming into the conference, I asked her how she was feeling. She said that something amazing had happened when she got out of bed that morning. For the first time in 12 years, when she put her feet on the floor, she could feel the cold floor. That weekend was a step in a new direction for me; I began to dream like a child again and to trust God in a whole new way.

His Kingdom, Your Adventure

Maybe you, like me, have been living your Christian life on grown-up faith. We trust God on one level, but we have difficulty entering into the present reality of His Kingdom because we have not yet returned to the childlike faith of our youth. I admit the majority of my Christian experience has been absent of this kind of faith. Though I would often verbally refer to God's power, I rarely saw the evidence of it in my daily life. Sadly, I believe my experience is all too common among Christians today.

What if God intends life in His Kingdom to be filled with impossible dreams and fantastic adventures? Could it be that the supernatural realities of the Kingdom of God are available to all those who will access them through childlike faith? Maybe Jesus' words about faith, the Kingdom, and supernatural living were true, not just for a few elite figures in history, but for regular people like you and me.

Could it be the reason our hearts beat faster and our adrenaline spikes when we imagine impossible adventures of heroic proportion is because we are being invited into the reality of such things? If the Kingdom of God was intended to be filled with supernatural adventure, why is it that, for many of us, our lives are absent of the miraculous? In our journey, we have discovered, though the Kingdom is present and available to all of God's children, many of us live our lives as if it is not.

Sleepy Christians

12

The Limits Of Logic

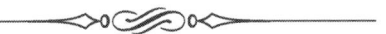

**Many of the questions we ask God can't be answered
directly, not because God doesn't know the answers,
but because our questions don't make sense. As C.S.
Lewis once pointed out, many of our questions are,
from God's point of view, rather like someone
asking, "Is yellow square or round? or "How
many hours are there in a mile?"**

N.T. Wright

I can't logically explain how God created the entire universe out of
absolutely nothing. It is beyond my ability to comprehend how there
could be an end to outer space. After all, if outer space ends, what's
beyond that, more space, I guess? I am completely baffled by the
intricacies of color and detail on the multitudes of insects and birds on
planet Earth. It's like each was hand painted in detail with an extremely
small paint brush.

My brain hurts when I consider the thought that God has
ALWAYS existed – forever and ever. How can that be? How can
anything eternally exist? Where did He (God) come from? And, what is
"time" anyway? Where did it come from? When did time begin? What
would happen if time ends? Will it end? Would I want it to end? How
can anything exist outside of time?

My mind is blown by the thought of our fragile human existence on a piece of ground that sits at exactly the right distance from our sun so life can be sustained. If we were any closer we would burn up from the heat; slightly farther and we would freeze from the cold. Paul reminds us that Jesus created all things and "holds all things together" (Col 1:17). How does He do that? What will happen if He lets go? In reality, when considering everything we humans do not know, it seems a bit arrogant to admit that we really know much of anything, comparatively speaking. Job sums up the matter well by saying:

> *Where can wisdom be found?*
> *Where does understanding dwell?*
> *No mortal comprehends its worth;*
> *it cannot be found in the land of the living.*
>
> *Job 28:12-13*

Despite our complete dependence on God for our existence and the extreme limitlessness of our inability to understand, many of us still live our lives almost completely dependent upon logic and reasoning, a byproduct of the enlightenment and our Greek education, I suppose. I admit I lived my Christian life this way for many years, limiting my faith to what I could comprehend.

I remember having a conversation with a lady in the checkout at the grocery store several years ago. She told me that God had instantly healed her of a terminal disease through the prayers of a well-known "faith healer." I smiled and said, "Wow, that's great." After she left, I thought, she was either lying or crazy. Somehow, I couldn't accept what I could not understand. I had developed a theological bias against anything I couldn't explain.

The Problem with Logic

The problem with logic is, when left to itself, it places limits on our faith that exclude any possibility of the supernatural. Remember, faith does not come from the mind, it comes from the heart. "For it is with your heart that you believe..." (Romans 10:10). If we rely solely on our reasoning capacity and fail to invite God to reveal truth beyond our capacity to comprehend, we will reject or deny the power of God in our lives. There is a limit to the amount of revelation we can receive from God through logic and reason alone. Dallas Willard explains,

The eternal life of which Jesus speaks is not knowledge about God, but an intimately interactive relationship with Him.

It's not that God is opposed to logic. He has created us with a tremendous ability to reason and problem solve. The difficulty arises when we close ourselves off to the supernatural and trust exclusively in our reasoning ability.

An honest look at Jesus' interaction with the disciples reveals that He was a bit put out on several occasions when His disciples would not believe in the possibility for the miraculous. This is magnified by the fact that they had already observed the same miraculous events on several occasions. His frustration rose from the fact that the disciples were not coupling reason with faith, especially when faith required them to accept what they could not understand. Much of the Church today lives with a similar mental block for the supernatural.

In my personal journey, I often spoke a lot about God's sovereignty and power in theory, but rejected everything that hinted of the miraculous. I was comfortable with the idea that God had revealed His great power in the past and was fine with the possibility of God showing His power in the future. However, to speak of Him showing His power among us today would have been borderline heresy from my theological perspective. I had somehow developed a theological system that allows for the miraculous to occur in any time period except for our own.

Many of us have grown up believing that we can't trust what we can't see. Though Jesus clearly taught otherwise, this concept has become thoroughly rooted in Christian thought over the past century. We have come to believe that we can trust our brain, but we can't trust spiritual intuition. We have argued against any form of subjective revelation without acknowledging that the very art of discerning the Word of God is also a subjective process. It requires the use of our imaginations to picture the theological truths expressed in Scripture.

When our physical minds are elevated above spiritual intuition, our dreams, or rather God's dreams for us, become limited to what our brains determine to be logical. Jesus said that true worshippers must learn to worship in both "spirit and truth" (John 4:23). The Greek word *pneuma* in this verse is a reference to the human spirit, not the Holy Spirit of God. Worshipping God is not an exclusively intellectual journey of our brains; it is also a journey of our spirits (hearts).

Without the involvement of our spirit, God's involvement with our imagination is severed, and our expectation is diminished to logic alone. The miraculous is then relegated to the realm of fantasy. We then become practical atheists who believe in a miraculous God but never expect anything out of the ordinary from Him. When God fails to perform, or better, performs down to our expectations, we develop theological systems to explain His inactivity.

Logic and the E.R.

One day, not long ago, I was on my way to a meeting when I heard God say (not audibly), "Turn left and go to the hospital emergency room." Everything inside of me replied, "That's not logical God." I was already running late for my meeting, the hospital was out of the way, and I had no logical reason to go there. Nevertheless, I felt strongly that God was prompting me.

I pulled into a parking spot, turned off the engine and quickly prayed something like: "Ok God, why am I here?" As I focused my heart on God's love, these words came to my mind: girl, wrist, and mom. As ridiculous and illogical as it seemed, I grabbed a receipt from my wallet and wrote these words on the back. I reached for a book that I had been reading, stuck the receipt inside and headed for the hospital entrance.

When I walked into the E.R., there was no one in sight apart from the attendant at the front desk. Confused and a little irritated, I turned to leave. As I headed for the exit doors, I once again sensed God telling me to sit down and read my book. I hadn't read but a few pages when a girl and her sister walked into the E.R., she was holding her wrist. I thought something to the effect, "OK God, here we go again." After she had checked in, I gathered the courage to ask her what was wrong. She had a visible lump on her wrist and had been in pain for a couple of days.

I pulled the receipt from my book and showed it to the girl. I said, "This might sound crazy, but God sent me here to pray for you. He must really love you." I showed her the words on the receipt. When she saw the words I had written, tears filled her eyes. As we talked, I discovered that on top of her wrist condition, her mom was in congestive heart failure. She greatly needed an encounter with God's love. As I prayed for her, I asked God to bring comfort and peace to her and her family. I also prayed for healing for her mom and her wrist.

When we finished praying, she looked down at her wrist. The lump had nearly disappeared, and the pain was gone. She moved it around in disbelief. At that point, the nurse called her name to be seen by the doctor. She said, "What should I do? I don't need to go back there anymore." I said, "Why don't you go tell the doctor what God has done for you today?" She smiled, we hugged like family, and she walked away with the nurse. As I left the hospital, once again, I thought something like, "God, you are so crazy... Crazy good."

Sleepy Christians

13

God Likes Pictures

**Faith consists in believing
when it is beyond the power of reason to believe.**

Voltaire

Throughout Scripture, God often intervened to open the spiritual eyes of His servants so they could see a reality invisible to their natural eyes. There is a great story that illustrates this in the Old Testament. The King of Aram became angry with the prophet Elisha and sent a great number of chariots and soldiers to capture Elisha in the city of Dothan. When Elisha and his servant woke up in the morning, they were surrounded by a vast army prepared for battle. Here is the account in II Kings:

When the servant of the man of God got up and went out early the next morning, an army with horses and chariots had surrounded the city. The servant cried out, "Oh, no, my lord! What shall we do?" the servant asked. "Don't be afraid," the prophet answered. "Those who are with us are more than those who are with them." And Elisha prayed, "Open his eyes, Lord, so that he may see." Then the Lord opened the servant's eyes, and he looked and saw the hills full of horses and chariots of fire all around Elisha.

2 Kings 6:15-17

The account of Elisha and his servant presents a clear picture of how God intends imagination and logical reasoning to operate together. It was completely logical for Elisha's servant to panic when he saw the vast enemy army with his physical eyes; rational thinking would expect nothing less. However, it would have been completely unreasonable for the servant to panic after his spiritual eyes were opened to the reality of God's superior army. Logic is overruled when God reveals a greater reality.

Our Imagination is God's Canvas

Just as God opened the spiritual eyes of Elisha's servant, He often uses the canvas of our imaginations to reveal realities we are unable to see with our natural eyes. The problem for me was, that I was largely closed off to the possibility of attaining revelation in this way. As a result, reasoning became my only means of gaining revelation from God. The result, of course, is the miraculous vanishes from our lives and we are left perplexed and unbelieving when faced with anything beyond the mundane and ordinary. Paul prayed for spiritual awakening to occur among the Ephesians:

> *I pray also that the eyes of your heart may be enlightened in order that you may know the hope to which he has called you, the riches of his glorious inheritance in his holy people, and his incomparably great power for us who believe.* That power is the same as the mighty strength he exerted when he raised Christ from the dead and seated him at his right hand in the heavenly realms, far above all rule and authority, power and dominion, and every name that is invoked, not only in the present age but also in the one to come. And God placed all things under his feet and appointed him to be head over everything for the church, which is his body, the fullness of him who fills everything in every way.   *Ephesians 1:18-23*

Notice, Paul wants the Ephesians to see something spiritually that they are unable to see with their physical eyes in hopes that they will understand something they cannot comprehend through human logic and reasoning alone. Paul refers to the spiritual eyes as "the eyes of your heart" and places great value on using both logic and spiritual intuition to discern God's will.

I have grown to love the process of understanding and applying the Word of God to my daily life. I believe that the Scriptures were birthed by the Spirit and are essential to life in the Kingdom (II Tim 3:16). However, a commitment to the Scriptures doesn't replace the need to receive spiritual revelation directly from the Holy Spirit. The Apostle Paul often spoke of our need for spiritual revelation. To the Corinthians, he writes:

"What no eye has seen, what no ear has heard, and what no human mind has conceived the things God has prepared for those who love Him. These are the things God has revealed to us by His Spirit. The Spirit searches all things, even the deep things of God. For who knows a person's thoughts except their own spirit within them? In the same way, no one knows the thoughts of God except the Spirit of God. What we have received is not the spirit of the world, but the Spirit who is from God, so that we may understand what God has freely given us. This is what we speak, not in words taught us by human wisdom, but in words taught by the Spirit, explaining spiritual realities with Spirit-taught words.   *I Cor 2:9-13*

God Likes Pictures

One day a while back, our family was in line at Arby's to order lunch. As I neared the front of the line, a strange thing occurred. I was looking at the menu above the girl at the checkout when all the sudden a picture of a video took over my mind. I was simply trying to order my lunch but the picture of the cover of this video made it difficult to see the menu. The video was a documentary about the miraculous things that God is doing around the world.

When it was my turn to order, I just said, "Hey, have you ever seen the video…" and then I mentioned the name of the video. The girl stopped and looked at me as if I were from Mars and then she said something like, "Yes, I watched that video last night and I wondered if it's true that God still does that stuff." I said something like, "Yes, He still does that stuff, in fact, He just did." I then explained to her why I had asked her the question in the first place. This encounter impacted her so much that she came out to talk with us while we ate our lunch. God loves people and He will use any means necessary to let them know, even a picture of a video cover.

There are truths and spiritual realities that are far beyond our ability to comprehend. We access these Kingdom realities through reason and imaginative childlike faith. Some may object, "You can't trust your imagination or spiritual revelation because it is subjective and may lead you astray." However, the study and interpretation of Scripture is also a subjective process, yet few would suggest that we should stop reading our Bibles. Both the study of God's Word and spiritual discernment are necessary to life in the Kingdom.

Though the Spirit does not speak contrary to the written Word of God, He is not limited by the written Word in what He reveals to men. It is the dynamic interplay of God's written Word and His direct interaction with His children that leads them into all truth. Through the written Word, the Holy Spirit awakens us to Heaven's realities and then moves us to go out and do the impossible.

This entire discussion leads us back to Jesus' words, "Unless you become like a little child, you will never see the Kingdom of God." What is childlike faith? Is faith simply the act of believing what we have the capacity to understand? Is it limited to reason apart from spiritual discernment? Paul defined faith in this way, "Now faith is the substance of things hoped for, the evidence of things not seen..." (Hebrews 11:1) We often define faith as believing in what we have learned and have come to understand as truth. We accept the truth that Jesus is the Son of God and accept His sacrifice as payment for our sins.

Limiting our faith to what we can understand leaves us heavy on information, but light on encounter. We end up with a reasonable faith, but not a supernatural one. Instead, Paul says that there is substance to our faith. The kind of faith we are called to have (childlike faith) results in something. This "something" is not just a golden ticket to enter Heaven someday when we die. Faith is the substance of the Kingdom of God taking place now, here on Earth. Faith is the currency of Heaven, bringing forth Kingdom realities into the present realm of our Earthly existence. Through faith, the children of God have access to the supernatural realities of His Kingdom. Hebrews 11 makes this abundantly clear:

> *And what more shall I say? I do not have time to tell about Gideon, Barak, Samson, and Jephthah, about David and Samuel and the prophets, who through faith conquered kingdoms, administered justice, and gained what was promised; who shut the mouths of lions, quenched the fury of the flames, and escaped the edge of the sword; whose weakness was turned to strength; and who became powerful in battle and routed foreign armies. Women received back their dead raised to life again. There were others who were tortured, refusing to be released so that they might gain an even better resurrection. Some faced jeers and flogging and even chains and imprisonment. They were put to death by stoning; they were sawed in two; they were killed by the sword. They went about in sheepskins and goatskins, destitute, persecuted and mistreated— the world was not worthy of them. They wandered in deserts and mountains, living in caves and in holes in the ground.* Hebrews 11:32-38

When God speaks or paints Heaven's realities on the canvas of our imaginations and we act upon them, the Kingdom of Heaven is opened to us. When we see the Kingdom through childlike faith and act through courage, we are then able to step into it and encounter its realities. When we encounter Heaven's realities, we are then required to operate within the realm of revelation that God has opened to us. It doesn't make sense to continue operating in the former reality any longer, regardless of how logical it may seem.

Though logic is a huge part of the discernment process, logic must submit to revelation when God opens our eyes to a greater reality. If we reject all revelation that we cannot understand, we will miss the supernatural aspects of the Kingdom of God. As Gordon Fee aptly states:

> *My concern is that in our having His Spirit, we not settle for a watered-down understanding that gives more glory to Western rationalism and spiritual anemia than to the Living God.*

Faith Beyond Reason

Maybe you, like me, have had Jesus "stuck in your head" for the greater part of your Christian life. Maybe you, too, have limited encounters with God to those acceptable experiences that fit safely within the confines of your understanding or comprehension. Logic is a gift to us from an intelligent and all-knowing creator, but He never intended logic to limit our expectation for the miraculous. If we fail to partner logic with faith, we end up with a reasonable religious existence absent of the supernatural realities of Heaven. If you struggle trusting God beyond what you can logically understand, maybe today would be a good day to ask Jesus for help in this area.

14

Does God Still Do That?

**We have so persistently dissembled the power of the
Gospel… that it is pardonable if those who judge
of it by us should doubt whether it is anything
more efficacious and inspiring than the pathetic
guesses which adorn the writings of philosophy.**

Canon B.F. Westcott

Some of our favorite family reading is the series by C.S. Lewis – The Chronicles of Narnia. One story we have read several times is "The Lion, the Witch, and the Wardrobe." In this story, four children - Peter, Susan, Edmund, and Lucy - discover a passageway from our world into another world called "Narnia" by way of a wardrobe in the professor's house. Lucy discovered the magical passageway while playing a game of hide-and-seek with the others and was followed later by her brother, Edmund.

Although Lucy and Edmund spend the better part of a day in Narnia, when they return through the passageway in the wardrobe, only a few moments had passed in our world. Lucy relayed the story of her fantastic adventure to her older siblings, Peter and Susan, but, of course, they thought she was only telling an elaborate story. Edmund, who had also been to Narnia, denied it because the white witch had deceived him. Edmund made fun of Lucy and agreed with the others that she was acting childish by pretending to believe in such things.

Later, Peter and Susan went to the professor to discuss their concern about Lucy. They believed she was carrying the fantasy about Narnia too far and wouldn't let it go. Peter and Susan relayed the whole story to the professor, telling him of Lucy's fanciful imaginations of Narnia, Tumnus the Faun, the white witch and more. To their surprise, the professor replied, "How do you know that your sister is not telling the truth?" After a discussion that lasted for some time, the professor determined that Lucy was neither lying nor delusional. He reasoned that the only logical conclusion was that Lucy had, in fact, been telling the truth about Narnia and the magical wardrobe.

Although it seemed contrary to reason, Peter and Susan began to entertain thoughts that a supernatural world of miraculous adventure, though invisible, must exist after all. The world of God's Kingdom is much like the land of Narnia described by C.S. Lewis. Though most Christians believe that God's Kingdom exists in some form or fashion, they live their daily lives as if this realm has no consequence on their present existence. I, for one, had almost no expectation that anything miraculous or supernatural had much to do with God's present Kingdom or my Christian walk.

Does God Still Do That?

In our family prayer to have "more of God," we were not expecting anything miraculous or supernatural. We were not in pursuit of miracles, healing or signs, and wonders from God. Nothing like this was on our radar at that point. One of the theological papers I had written in seminary was on the topic of "miracles and the sign gifts." After ninety pages of reasoned eloquence, my conclusion was that the "sign" gifts and all miracles ended with the completion of the New Testament Canon or the passing of the apostolic era.

I have since come to believe that a lack of the miraculous among God's people is more the result of a theological phenomenon within the Church in recent years than a true reflection of God's inactivity. As we began to experience more of God's presence, we also began to see more of His power. It seems that God's presence and power are somewhat of a package deal. If you get more of God's presence, you get more of His power as well.

A "Journey" Into Miracles

When we began experiencing God's love and power in greater ways, miracles began to occur somewhat regularly in our family and church. Our children and teens began praying for their friends, and healing began to occur in youth group meetings and the children's ministry. We also started experiencing supernatural healing at some of the conferences we were attending during this time. We began seeing God heal people in public, as well in the most unlikely of places, like Wal-Mart, Dairy Queen, the ER, Urgent Care or one of the local restaurants. The miraculous began to occur frequent enough that some people at our conservative evangelical church became a bit uncomfortable.

It was evident that the topic of the miraculous needed to be addressed on Sunday morning with our entire congregation, but I was still in process myself. I remember reluctantly starting off the New Year with a series entitled, "Does God Still Do That?" In the series, I addressed a lot of questions, took a fresh look at the Scriptural basis for the miraculous and tried, as best I could, to humbly admit to our church family that I had neglected to teach on the miraculous nature of the Kingdom or the presence of God.

It's Not All about Miracles

If you are from a theological background similar to mine, I can almost guess at the questions that you are asking right now, probably something like: "Yeah, but it's not all about miracles, right? After all, miracles are temporary. We're all gonna die eventually anyway. Why should we focus on such temporary (Earthly) things? Isn't it selfish or self-serving to want to see a miracle or healing? Maybe God intends to use some sickness, disease, etc., to build character in our lives."

These are common thoughts that would enter my mind whenever I heard someone talking about God, healing, and miracles. However, I now believe that questions like these reflect a misunderstanding of God's heart and that God desires to free His children from the bondage and brokenness in their lives, including physical sickness and disease; more on this in a minute.

It was a pursuit of God's presence and not a pursuit of His power that brought about the shift in our thinking which eventually led to a shift in our experience. When Tara and I became convinced that God still does today what He did in the early Church, we began to pray with greater expectancy. We also began to teach our children about God's willingness to heal. We shared Bible stories about healing and the miraculous things done by Jesus and the disciples. We also told them that Jesus wanted to use them in miraculous ways, just as He used the people in the Bible.

Tara and I learned a lot from our children during this season of our journey because, in some ways, their childlike faith allowed them greater access to God's Kingdom than we had access to at that point. They simply believed like children and did what God said they could do. There is nothing quite like the innocent faith of children. As I grow older, I hope to become more and more like them.

Over the past several years, we have seen God do many things that are not easily understood from the vantage point of logic. At one time, I would have argued something like this, "Though God is sovereign and can do whatever He chooses, He has sovereignly chosen not to do miraculous things today." I would then present various practical and theological reasons to explain God's inactivity. "After all," I reasoned, "It's for our own good that God keeps the miraculous realm from us."

I believed that God was keeping miracles from us to prevent us from being distracted or from becoming puffed up with pride. Through logic and a bit of theological training, I was comfortably able to justify my position with reasoned arguments from Scripture and history.

An Encounter with Jaws

One night, several years ago, at a conference I was brought face to face with my theological hang-ups with the miraculous. During a time of prayer for healing, I was asked to pray for a woman with severe jaw problems. She had a TMJ disorder that had been worsened by failed surgeries. When we talked about her condition, she had difficulty speaking and her jaw was clearly misaligned.

As I placed my hand on her jaw and began to pray, though I was hopeful, I wasn't overcome with expectation that anything supernatural would occur. Immediately, I felt a flow of electrical current between my hand and her jaw. My nephew, who was praying with us, placed his hand on my hand and felt the current as well. The lady began to cry and expressed that she also felt heat in her jaw. Within a few moments, her jaw had popped into place, and she was pain free. We were all overwhelmed and amazed at God's goodness. The lady called her husband to tell him what had occurred, talking with clarity and ease.

Miracles Reveal God's Love

Having had many similar encounters since that day, I am not only convinced that miracles happen, but that God intends for them to be part of the normal Christian life. We have seen God heal many injuries and sicknesses over the past several years. Some healing has been instant; some has occurred over time through continued prayer. It has become evident when God heals or performs a miracle that it's not primarily about His desire to reveal His power. If it was God's sole purpose to showcase His power, He could choose much more dramatic displays. The creator of the universe could easily blow up a mountain with an asteroid or shake the Earth with His voice to display His great power.

Miracles, more than a display of God's power, are a display of His love. In fact, miracles are part of God's nature; they are no big deal for Him. God loves people so much that He will do anything to show them how much He cares for them. Healing is just another way God reveals His relentless love and compassion to people. So, in relation to miracles, if you ever find yourself wondering, "does God still do that?" The answer is, yes, absolutely He does, and He invites you to participate in expressing His love in this way.

Sleepy Christians

15

Where Did All The Miracles Go?

**Miracles are a retelling in small letters of the very same
story which is written across the whole world
in letters too large for some of us to see.**

C.S. Lewis

I used to be offended by what I would see on television, the
ostentatious show that is often made of Jesus and the ministry of
healing. In all honesty, I still cringe a bit by ministry styles and Christian
marketing pleas that seem to run contrary to the character and humble
nature of Jesus, but I no longer allow the abuses to distract me from the
reality of God's goodness.

Satan, the deceiver, is the author of confusion. He loves to
counterfeit what God does and then make a mockery of it. I am not
implying that all ministry styles that I am uncomfortable with are the
work of the devil. However, the devil has been known to counterfeit or
distort God's work in order to cause confusion or disbelief in the
supernatural. I have come to believe that it's not wise to reject what we
see just because it makes us uncomfortable or defies our understanding.
The devil often uses our offense to keep us from the full reality of God's
Kingdom. Also, I have learned to relax a bit and stop being the judge
and jury for which ministries are walking in truth and which are not.

Discontinuity and the Miraculous

If theological discussion causes you to zone out or lose consciousness, feel free to bypass the next few pages. For those interested, this section will attempt to briefly address the theological basis that has often been presented in opposition to present-day miracles.

The most unfortunate theological teaching of fundamental evangelicalism is the doctrine of cessationism. I understand the reasoning behind this theology since I once taught it myself; however, I have since come to believe that this view misrepresents Scripture. Though not universal, it has been increasingly taught over the past one hundred years that miracles and the supernatural "sign" gifts ceased with the completion of the New Testament canon, or the passing of the apostolic era. It is, therefore, suggested that these gifts are no longer available to believers within the Church today. In the case of liberal theology, it's often taught that miracles have never existed in church history and so the existence of present-day miracles is rejected as well.

Among Evangelical Christians, the Dispensational model has served equally well to dismiss the miraculous from the Church today. Ironically, the topic of my master's Thesis was "Covenantal and Dispensational Views of Church." To show that I am not throwing stones, I want to share up front that I believe dispensational thinkers have contributed significantly to a theology of the New Testament Church, and an understanding of the relationship between the Biblical Covenants. Also, not everyone who holds to a dispensational theological model rejects the miraculous or the present use of the sign gifts.

I also believe that there is merit in understanding the discontinuity between the Old and New Testaments. Dispensational thinkers have contributed significantly in helping the Church to understand the radical newness that came through Christ. The New Testament, in many respects, is the record of a new dispensation of God's activity on Planet Earth and presents a clear distinction between Israel and the Church. In addressing what I believe to be excess, I do not intend to communicate that the dispensational model is without merit. I also acknowledge that dispensationalism is only one contributing factor to a reduced expectancy of the miraculous today.

However, since Dispensationalism presents a system that views God working differently throughout progressive eras in redemptive history, it follows logically that this theological system can be used to explain a lack of supernatural expectation within the Church today. The logic goes something like this; "God is not working miracles today, especially through people, because we have moved beyond the time period of miracles into a new dispensation in redemptive history."

I do not believe that Scripture supports the conclusions of some dispensational writers regarding miracles, signs, and wonders. God has not ceased from His supernatural activities and "moved on" to another phase in His redemptive plan; this becomes evident when we consider that miracles reflect the goodness and mercy of God toward humanity and are an inherent part of His nature. The difficulty, in my opinion, is that some dispensational writers have used the "theme" of discontinuity to support conclusions about miracles and the sign gifts that are neither biblical nor consistent with Church history.

The Miraculous and Church History

Some, from my background, have proposed that the Bible and Church history support the view that miracles were isolated to a couple brief time periods, namely the time periods of the Old Testament prophets and the New Testament Apostles. However, an honest look at history reveals this to be inaccurate.

In this light, Jack Deere, former professor at Dallas Theological Seminary, in his book "Surprised by the Power of the Spirit," outlines an abundance of miraculous activity throughout the entirety of the Old and New Testaments. Neither Scripture nor an honest look at Church history support the theological stance that God limited His miraculous intervention to brief time periods in history.

I understand, there have been time periods within Church history when miracles were far less common. From my perspective, this is not an indication of God's inactivity, but a reflection on the poor doctrinal and spiritual condition of the Church during these times. Also, the lack of miraculous events coming out of the Reformation can be viewed more as a response to the abuses within the existing Church than a true reflection of God's unwillingness to do mighty things, kind of a "throw the baby out with the bathwater" mentality. The supernatural nature of the Kingdom has always been available to those who access it through faith.

Miracles – What's New?

Throughout history and without interruption, miracles have marked the presence of a supernatural God actively involved among His people. In the seminary paper that I mentioned earlier, I presented several reasons why I believed miracles are rare and why the sign gifts (tongues, prophecy, healings, words of knowledge, etc.) are no longer in operation in the Church. At the time, I believed that my arguments were solid and that Scripture supported my conclusions.

Not long ago, I reread my paper and realized that much of what I had written was based on "eisegesis" not "exegesis." Exegesis is the study of Scripture in its original context with the intent of discovering the truths of what the authors were attempting to communicate to their audience. Eisegesis is coming to the text of Scripture with an agenda, something to prove, then somehow finding that meaning in the text, even if it's not really there.

I realized that much of my paper, if I'm honest, was written with the intention of proving the sign gifts had ceased, that miracles are rare, and that God doesn't work His wonders through ordinary people today. I was guilty of doing the very thing my professors had taught me not to do by reading my own conclusions into Scripture instead of allowing Scripture to speak for itself. Unfortunately, this process has been fairly common throughout Church history. The truth is, much of modern scholarship regarding the miraculous has been somewhat reactionary against some of the abuse that has taken place within the Church.

Historically, Christians have justified bigotry, slavery, genocide and many other atrocities in the name of Jesus. We have often justified our actions through our interpretations of Scripture. I am not implying that all misinterpretation of the Scripture is of evil intent. Most of us approach Scripture with every intention of correctly handling the Word of God. I am only attempting to highlight the importance of allowing the Bible to speak for itself rather than subtly, even unknowingly, using the Bible to support conclusions we already embrace.

Being Honest with the Scriptures

Something occurred to me one day as I was working my way through some passages of Scripture that I once used to argue against the present existence of the miraculous. If one hundred new believers, with no prior theological training, were given a Bible and sent away for six months to study the Scriptures alone with no external influence or teaching apart from the Holy Spirit, what would they conclude about miracles and the sign gifts?

I believe most, if not all, would return believing from Scripture that God still performs miracles today and that He intends for miracles to be a normal part of the Christian life. I don't believe an honest, unbiased study of the Scriptures will lead one to conclude that the sign gifts have ceased or that miracles are unavailable to the Church today.

Another thought occurred to me during this process. Many of my conclusions were based largely on my experience, or lack of experience, rather than an honest evaluation of what God has said. It was difficult for me to conclude that the sign gifts were still operative today when I wasn't experiencing them myself. My conclusions were just a reflection of my lack of faith couched in theological language.

I was reluctant to admit that miracles were still part of God's routine when they were anything but routine in my life. This poses a dilemma for many pastors and Christian leaders, including myself, since acknowledging these truths would not only violate what we have believed, but what we have taught others for many years.

Sleepy Christians

16

Miracles And Ordinary People

**God delights to delegate His power to men,
when He can find believing and obedient
servants to accept and exercise it.**

John A. MacMillan

One of the most wonderfully surprising practices of God is how He consistently chooses to use ordinary people in extraordinary ways. It's in God's nature to use average joe's to accomplish His purposes and to advance His Kingdom. This was true throughout Scripture and it is still true today. Imagine that, God chooses to partner with His children rather than work His wonders apart from us.

The idea that God uses ordinary people in supernatural ways was one of the most difficult challenges I faced in my supernatural journey with God. How could God use an ordinary person like me to do supernatural things? My reasoning went something like this, "Jesus performed miracles, Jesus is God and, after all, I'm not Jesus; case closed."

Not long ago during our spring conference, I was once again reminded how God often uses ordinary people in extraordinary ways. After one session, a family from our church came forward seeking prayer for their young daughter. The little girl, now 1 year old, had been born deaf in both ears. Since the "professionals" were praying for others at the time, a small group of church folk gathered around her to pray. Within a short time, the little girl began responding to the voices and sounds around her; God had completely healed her ears. Shortly after the conference, doctors confirmed that her hearing was completely normal.

Believing that God still does miracles is one thing; believing that He wants us to participate, well that's another thing altogether. Like me, many believers pray and then wait for God to act independently of them. The New Testament, in contrast, reveals how God intends for His children to partner with Him in bringing His Kingdom to Earth.

When considering the supernatural nature of the Kingdom, we often fail to consider that God has taken up residence within us through the person of the Holy Spirit. Consider how much God must trust you to give you His Spirit. Consider the implications of hosting the presence of God. Francis Mac Nutt writes:

> For the first 350 years, the leaders of the early Church taught that every Christian could heal the sick and even cast out evil spirits.

It's not God's intention to bring Heaven to Earth apart from us but through us. Paul writes, "We are therefore Christ's ambassadors, as though God were making His appeal through us" (2 Corinthians 5:20). As His ambassadors, we represent Him to the world. We say exactly what He would say, and we do exactly what He would do.

The word disciple means to copycat or mimic. Mimicking Him is possible because His presence dwells within us. Though we get to participate with Him, it's God's power working through us that accomplishes His purposes and reveals His relentless love. All glory belongs to Him, not us.

His Power In Our Weakness

Going a step further, God has given us a clear mission. He has given us the same mission He gave to Jesus. Jesus said, "Peace be with you! As the Father has sent me, I am sending you" (John 20:21). Our mission, like Jesus' mission, is to destroy the works of the devil (John 3:8) and to bring Heaven to Earth.

Jesus came to renew and restore everything the devil has stolen or disrupted in God's universe. To participate with Him, He has armed us with the power of His indwelling presence. Paul writes:

> *But we have this treasure in jars of clay to show that this all-surpassing power is from God and not from us.* *II Corinthians 4:7*

As humans, apart from His presence, we are weak and susceptible to the fallen world we inhabit. Our bodies are jars of clay, earthen vessels, dirt. When God's presence indwells our bodies, they become the vehicle to display His glory on the Earth. To the extent that we partner with Him and His Kingdom with our bodies, we become His hands and feet to bring restoration to our broken and wounded planet. His presence within us enables us to be used by Him to display His mighty works. Dallas Willard writes:

> *I believe men and women were designed by God, in the very constitution of their human personalities, to carry out His rule by meshing the relatively little power resident in their own bodies with the power inherent in the infinite Rule or Kingdom of God.*

It's our weaknesses that highlight that it's God's power at work and not our own. After all, we are cracked and broken vessels. The glory shining through us is clearly His glory, not our own. Paul explains this paradox by saying:

> *Now to Him who is able to do immeasurably more than all we ask or imagine, according to His power that is at work within us, to Him be glory in the Church and in Christ Jesus throughout all generations, forever and ever! Amen.* *Ephesians 3:20-21*

At one time, my reading of this passage limited the interpretation of God's powerful work within us to the change of life that comes through our relationship with Christ. Although I would agree that inner transformation is central to this passage, the greater context reveals that the purpose of God's work in us is to benefit and strengthen those around us.

Miracles—An All Play

Regardless of your experience, or lack of experience, with miraculous things, all of God's children have been equally invited to participate in His supernatural Kingdom. It was never God's intent that certain elite persons get to "play" while everyone else only gets to watch. The supernatural life is an "all play," and each one of us has been invited to participate. This is our God-given calling and destiny as children of the King. We are princes and princesses in His Kingdom, sharing together in the responsibility of bringing Heaven to Earth

In the Gospel of John, concerning the many great miracles He had performed, Jesus said these words to His disciples:

I tell you the truth, anyone who has faith in me will do what I have been doing.
He will do even greater things than these because I am going to the Father.
John 14:12

I once assumed the "anyone" in this verse didn't really mean anyone. Theologically, I would relegate the working of miracles to a few chosen individuals mentioned in Scripture. I love that Jesus didn't say "anyone who has faith and is a disciple" or "anyone who has faith and is an apostle" or "anyone who has faith and is a pastor." His only qualifier is that we have faith. Could this somehow include us? I believe it does.

Making Our Father Smile

I believe God gets super excited when His kids trust Him like children and take crazy risks fully expecting to see Heaven come to Earth. Just as we love to watch our kids kill fire-breathing dragons, capture evil villains, and bring peace back to the kingdom, our heavenly Father loves to watch as His children learn to trust Him for impossible things. We say to Him, "Daddy, will you?" And He says to us, "No, my child, you do it. It gives me great joy to watch you succeed."

Maybe your Christian walk, like mine, has been overly focused on what God is not doing. Is it possible that, due to the lack of supernatural occurrences in your life, you have concluded that God doesn't do miraculous things in His Church today? Or, if He does, they are extremely rare? Accepting that God still performs miracles today is essential to life in His supernatural Kingdom. After all, what is significant about a Kingdom that offers little or no expectation of the supernatural? How would this Kingdom differ from all other kingdoms that have existed on the Earth?

Maybe you have come to believe that, if God does use people in extraordinary ways today, He likely won't use you? However, as an apprentice of Jesus, God has entrusted you with His Spirit and given you the mandate to mimic the life of Jesus on Earth. Maybe today would be a good day to begin pursuing the mission God has entrusted to you – to renew and restore what the devil has stolen and destroyed.

A lack of the miraculous in our lives is not a sign of humility or balance. It is a reflection of unbelief in what God has clearly said about you and your role within His Kingdom today. You are His ambassador, sent to mimic Jesus to the world; you are to say what Jesus said and do what Jesus did.

Why not take some time to take a fresh look at the promises of Jesus, concerning miracles, throughout the New Testament. I believe you will discover that God has not ceased working miracles among His people nor from changing lives in supernatural ways. Perhaps it's time to rediscover the old truths about God spoken by Daniel when he said:

How great are His signs, how mighty His wonders! His Kingdom is an eternal Kingdom; His dominion endures from generation to generation.   *Daniel 4:3*

Have you ever wondered what God would say if He were still speaking today? Is it possible that He speaks to us far more than we think? In the following section, we will discuss the importance of hearing God's voice and sharing His words with others.

Sleepy Christians

17

The Wind, Tattoos & Baggage Claim

Without God's Spirit, there is nothing we can do that will count for God's Kingdom. Without God's Spirit, the Church simply can't be the Church.

N.T. Wright

One Fall morning, I traveled to the airport to pick up a speaker who was flying in for our Fall conference. His flight was very early in the morning, so I arrived at the airport around 6 am to pick him up. His plane had not yet landed, so I grabbed a seat by the luggage terminal to wait for him. The airport was almost desolate at that time of the morning with little activity apart from the rustle of a few airline employees.

I laid my head back against the seat, closed my eyes and tried to rest for a few minutes before the plane arrived. After a few moments, I felt a light breeze brush across my face. I had felt this breeze on other occasions and recognized it as God's attempt to gain my attention. When I opened my eyes, my heart sank. I knew what God was asking me to do.

Standing across from me at the baggage claim was a very rough-looking guy! He was large, had long, brown hair, a huge beard, and was completely covered in tattoos. He was wearing a shirt littered with expletives. On the back of his shirt, in large bold letters, it read, "Hail Satan." I quickly began a debate with God: "I can't talk with that guy,

God…anything I say will only make him angry…I don't even know what I would say."

Then I heard God say to my heart, "Talk to him about his father." So, with some reluctance, I walked over to him and said, "Hi! I was sitting over there, and I felt like God wanted me to come and share something with you." He looked at me with a bit of annoyance and said, "Well, I don't want to hear anything that He has to say." Gaining a little boldness, I said, "What if I tell you what I think He said, and if it's way off or doesn't make sense, you can just ignore it?" He reluctantly agreed.

As I began to speak, God gave me the words to say. I said something like, "You have been hurt by the people in your life who should have protected and cared for you – especially your father. Because your father is a religious person and has hurt you deeply, you think God must not love you either. You blame God for all the pain you have experienced in your life and have, therefore, pledged your allegiance to the devil. But it is the devil who wants to destroy your life and God who wants to save it…."

Although his face was toward the ground, I continued to share the words God gave me about his life. I saw tears slowly dripping from his beard. I told him how much God loved him and that He had never left him alone in his pain. I told him God was chasing after him and cared enough about him to get my attention by blowing in my face. I asked if I could pray for him and he nodded his head. After praying, we hugged like brothers who had not seen each other in years. When I left the airport with our speaker, I was overcome by God's goodness. What kind of God arranges a meeting between two strangers in an airport just to show His great love? I have yet to recover from that day!

Words from God?

Several years ago, Tara and I began having conversations with individuals who came up to us because they said they had been given "a word from the Lord" for us. This often occurred at a conference, church service, or some other Christian gathering. At the time we weren't sure what a "word from the Lord" was, and we certainly weren't expecting God to speak to us through some person we had never met, but we humored them anyway and listened to their "message from God."

At first, we didn't think much of it, but we began to realize that much of what was being spoken to us related directly to life situations that were personal and known only to our family. We were perplexed at how various people, who didn't know us or each other, could speak so clearly and specifically into our lives. We were given words about our church, our family, and our future that, were either true at the time, or have nearly all come to pass.

At one conference, three or four different people gave us a similar word regarding an awakening that was coming to our church. Some suggested there would be difficult times ahead for us, but that we should be encouraged because God was up to something good among us. We were encouraged that God's work among us was not a new thing but was just "more" of what He had been doing in our past. Most everything that was shared with us was relevant and specific to our current life circumstances. The crazy thing is, none of these people knew who we were, much less that we were church leaders. We were greatly moved by their words because we had been praying for more of God's love and presence in our lives.

Words that Make You Wonder

At one conference, a very large guy invited our family to dinner. We had seen him on several occasions before this point and had thought it odd that we kept running into him. As we sat together at dinner, he said he had been praying for me since the previous Christmas Eve when God had given him a vision for Ohio – and I was a part of that vision. I was not sure what to do with that. This guy gave some of the same prophetic words over our family that we had heard several times before and then he said something like: "And God is going to use your church to reach some of the ex-Amish Mennonites in your area."

I thought, "Nah, that can't be right. I don't know any ex-Amish Mennonites." God confirmed the word on a few other occasions when unrelated individuals gave us the same message about the ex-Amish Mennonites in our area. When we started our ministry school a year later, over forty ex-Amish Mennonites enrolled in our school.

My friend Vic, the big guy who gave the original word about the Mennonites, was present at the start of our ministry school. His eyes filled with tears as he saw the fruit of what God had said. But, then again, I have found him to be a big teddy bear anyway. Recently, a group has been gathering about an hour from our church for worship and fellowship.

Many of the members of this new gathering are graduates of the ministry school we started a few years back. In addition, a growing number of our current congregation are from an Amish or Mennonite background. Needless to say, from the fruit we have seen, I fully believe God speaks consistently and regularly through His children today.

As a Baptist pastor, if someone had approached me and told me that God had spoken to them or that they had heard His voice, I would have questioned their sanity or, at least, their honesty. The idea of God communicating apart from His written Word was outside of my theological comfort zone. I would often say, "God has spoken definitively through Scripture and is no longer speaking in that way today." Although I believed God directed in other ways, like closing doors or opening windows, I did not believe God still speaks directly and definitively to people today.

My reasoning was, if God is still speaking, then revelation is still occurring and the Canon of Scripture is, therefore, still open. Also, if the Canon of Scripture is still open, we have no final basis upon which to determine truth from error. After all, anyone could just say, "God told me…." and then whatever he or she says from that point forward carries the same weight as the written Word of God. From my limited view of revelation, accepting that God still speaks today would open the church to all sorts of heresy. It was easier to conclude that God's communication with us today is limited to His written Word and His vaguely discernible, still small voice.

What about the Sign Gifts?

Although my reasoning seemed sound, my conclusions were rooted in a misunderstanding of New Testament prophecy and a faulty belief that the sign gifts were unavailable to believers beyond the early Church.

One passage I had often used to support my belief that the sign gifts, including prophecy, were unavailable to believers in our day was in I Corinthians 13 – The love chapter. Following a discussion on the primacy of love, the Apostle Paul presents three gifts essential to life in the Kingdom that will no longer be needed in the life to come. The three gifts Paul mentions are words of knowledge, prophecy, and tongues. Paul writes:

> *Love never fails. But where there are prophecies, they will cease; where there are tongues, they will be stilled; where there is knowledge, it will pass away. For we know in part and we prophesy in part, but when completeness comes, what is in part disappears. When I was a child, I talked like a child, I thought like a child, I reasoned like a child. When I became a man, I put the ways of child- hood behind me. For now, we see only a reflection as in a mirror; then we shall see face to face. Now I know in part; then I shall know fully, even as I am fully known. Now, these three remain faith, hope & love, but the greatest of these is love.*   *I Corinthians 13:8-13*

I would often point out from this passage that Paul specifies a time when the sign gifts of tongues, prophecy and (words of) knowledge would no longer be necessary and would either cease altogether or slowly fade from usefulness. The passage specifies that "when completeness comes" (NIV) or "when that which is perfect comes" (KJV), there will no longer be a need for these supernatural gifts.

Evangelicals from my side of the tracks often suggest this occurred either at the completion of the Canon of Scripture or the close of the apostolic age. The reasoning goes something like this: the revelatory gifts are no longer necessary because the Word of God (a fuller and less subjective revelation of God's truth) has been completed. Pointing to this passage, I would sometimes suggest that reliance upon the sign gifts was childish now that we have the completed Scriptures. It was time to put the "ways of childhood" behind us and move on to a more substantial foundation.

Through time and study, it became increasingly difficult to maintain my position. For one, the idea that "when completeness comes" refers to the completion of the Canon or the close of the apostolic age goes directly against what Paul says. The passage clearly states that the time would come when we see Him "face to face." The context of the passage suggests that the sign gifts will continue until Jesus returns. The unanimous interpretation of the early Church fathers is in agreement with this conclusion.

When Jesus returns, the need for the gifts of prophecy, tongues, and words of knowledge will no longer exist since we can speak with Him directly, face to face. However, until Jesus' return, these gifts are necessary and essential to the growth, maturity, and edification of His body on Earth. Why would God remove, from the Church, such a vital and essential aspect of the growth and development of His body? I don't believe that He has or will until they are no longer necessary upon His reappearing.

18

Hearing & Sharing

———————⟨⟩————————

**To set our hearts on the Kingdom therefore means
to make the life of the Spirit within and among us
the center of all we think, say and do.**

Henri Nouwen

I'm not sure why I have always had such an aversion to the idea of God speaking to me. I suppose I always assumed that God typically only speaks to real prophets. You know, the ones clothed in a robe with a very long white beard, carrying a huge staff. Besides, it wasn't really a good idea for anyone within my theological circles to go around sharing that they had heard God speak to them. That kinda talk wouldn't get you a seat at the popular table.

Theologically, my lack of openness to hearing and sharing God's voice resulted from a misunderstanding of the nature and purpose of prophecy in the New Testament. I was afraid to share thoughts or words that I received from God because I was afraid, if I were wrong, I would make a fool of myself and bring dishonor to God. After all, Old Testament prophets were put to death for speaking presumptuously and proven wrong (Deuteronomy 18:20).

What I failed to realize is, in the Old Testament, the people of God were reliant upon the voice of God relayed through the prophets. God's Spirit had not yet been given to dwell within each believer. As a result, the prophet carried great authority because God spoke directly (audibly) to him, giving wisdom and direction to kings and nations.

Nations depended on the words of the prophet to be accurate since an incorrect or presumptuous word could result in calamity or defeat by foreign enemies. As a result, the penalty was severe for false prophets who lied about hearing the voice of God. The New Testament presents an added twist to the definition of prophecy. Though some are especially gifted, all believers have the privilege, even responsibility, of hearing and sharing God's voice with others.

In fact, Paul elevates prophecy above other gifts because of its usefulness in edifying the body. He writes, "Follow the way of love and eagerly desire spiritual gifts, especially the gift of prophecy" (I Corinthians 14:1). Though God may still speak audibly when He chooses, He also speaks to our spirits through His Spirit which He has placed within us. The New Testament ministry of prophecy is described by Paul in I Corinthians when he writes:

> *But the one who prophesies speaks to people for their strengthening, encouraging and comfort.*   *I Corinthians 14:3*

Hearing and Sharing

Since each believer has been given the Spirit of God to dwell within them, hearing God's voice can and should become a normal part of our supernatural journey. Jesus said, "My sheep listen to my voice; I know them, and they follow me" (John 10:27). Tozer's words resonate with those of Jesus':

> *The soul has eyes with which to see and ears with which to hear. Feeble they may be from long disuse, but by the life-giving touch of Christ, they are now alive and capable of sharpest sight and most sensitive hearing.*

As we take time to be still and listen for His voice, we begin to perceive what He is saying. He may not speak audibly, and He may not speak English, but He will speak. Sometimes He will use words, but often He will not. Sometimes God may choose to communicate through pictures, thoughts, or feelings. The more we listen, the more we hear. The more we hear, the more we learn to identify His voice over competing voices.

Receiving or Perceiving?

The Old Testament prophets often heard God's voice audibly and simply repeated what they heard. Although God might still speak in this manner today, the New Testament believer also listens intently to hear the voice of the Holy Spirit. We do not always hear Him perfectly. Paul points out, we "prophesy in part, ...as through a darkened mirror."

Old Testament prophets *received* the direct verbatim word of the Lord. As New Testament believers, we *perceive* His words as His Spirit communicates with ours. When we hear His voice or receive words from others, we can then go to God alone to ask for confirmation. Often, God will gently confirm the word we have heard, or He will send others to confirm the word we have received.

Learning to Hear

Learning to hear God's voice and respond to what He says is a process we grow in as we progress in our supernatural journey with God. Though I was often expressive in my conversation with God, rarely was it my practice to set aside time to listen for His words of encouragement, love, and direction. Eugene Peterson writes, "If we pray without listening, we pray out of context."

I, like so many others, was an "out of context" prayer. Also, if I had heard God speak, I certainly wouldn't have approached others saying I believed it to be a "word" directly from the mind of God. A huge part of my transformation came from realizing that God still speaks to His children today and we can hear His voice if we are tuned in and listening intently.

When we hear God's voice, it fills us with faith to say and do as He leads. We then begin to live our lives communicating the Gospel through our words and actions, often through supernatural means. Jesus said, "I only do what I see the Father doing" (John 5:19). He taught us, by example, that prayer is an intimate interaction with our loving Heavenly Father. It is the intimate exchange of listening and speaking, seeing and perceiving, giving and receiving that helps us to understand His will and enables us to help accomplish it on Earth as in Heaven.

Josie's Word

Not long ago, our family traveled to Michigan for a conference. We were in a "breakout" session with about a hundred other people when our youngest daughter, Josie, was invited to the front of the room to give a "word from God." Josie was seven at the time, and this kind of thing was very new to our family. I was nervous for her, but Josie took the microphone and said something like, "There is a little girl here named Gracie and God wants to heal you today."

I thought to myself, "Nice try Josie, but you should have picked a more common name than Gracie. There is no way there is a Gracie in this small group, especially in need of healing." The facilitator asked if there was a Gracie in the room. There was no response. Nevertheless, he graciously offered a prayer for "Gracie," and then the workshop ended.

Following the workshop, while standing around by the restrooms, we overheard a mother say to her child, "Do you want a drink of water, Gracie?" Our eyes got big, and my daughters ran over to pray with this little girl who was bound to her wheelchair. Gracie had come to the conference with her parents. She had a disease that hindered her brain from properly firing which prevented her from walking normally. Gracie had been in the breakout session, but her mother had taken her out to use the restroom before Josie shared her "word from God."

That evening Gracie was the last person prayed for during a time of prayer for healing. Although there were signs that God's presence had impacted her, we were unsure if she had received healing from God on that night. One year later, at a conference at the same location, we saw Gracie again. She was no longer confined to her wheelchair, and she was walking, with some help, yet with relative ease! I am still unable to fully wrap my mind around things like this.

Have you, like me, been somewhat closed off to the voice of God because you haven't really expected Him to say anything to you? Maybe you have concluded, like many others, that God is no longer speaking to His children the way He once did. Maybe, on occasion, you have heard His voice clearly, but have been reluctant to share what He has said because you were afraid of speaking presumptuously on His behalf. "After all," you might add, "the gift of prophecy has been abused and misused within the Church in recent years." Though this statement contains some truth, it is also true for every gift the Holy Spirit has given to the Church. It seems that we play into the devil's hand when we fail to operate in one of God's gifts simply because some abuse or misuse it.

I believe that Tozer is right in saying, "God is not silent, has never been silent. It is the very nature of God to speak." God desires His children to listen intently for His voice and share His words with others to bring them strength, encouragement, and edification. If you struggle with the idea of hearing God's voice or have been reluctant to share His words, today might be a good day to begin an adventure of hearing and sharing. May our longing for God's voice grow to the point that we can say as Jesus did, "Man shall not live by bread alone, but on every word that comes from the mouth of God" (Matthew 4:4).

Sleepy Christians

19

All Words, No Power

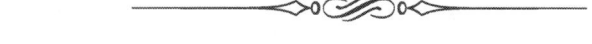

**God's looking for people through whom He can do the
impossible. What a pity that we plan
only things we can do by ourselves.**

A.W. Tozer

I used to take great pride in my ability to use reasonable arguments in presenting the Gospel message to doubters, unbelievers, and agnostics. I loved to debate philosophy, theology, or anything else I felt adequately trained to argue about. I had a ready defense when it came to the Gospel, and I constantly looked for opportunities to prove it. What frustrated me the most was, for many, my answers weren't enough to convince them that the Gospel was true or that Jesus was who He claimed to be.

Eloquently Worded Arguments

I remember having a lengthy conversation with a brilliant homeless guy from Cincinnati one Friday evening while on a ministry outreach in college. The more I used logic and reason to try and convince him of my ideas, the less interested he became in what I had to say. It's not that I failed to offer answers to his questions; it's just that my answers were not enough to convince him that what I believed about Jesus and the Bible was true. Then, as I had been taught to do, I pulled the trump card;

I began to share truths about Jesus' resurrection.

I shared the biblical and historical evidence showing, beyond a reasonable doubt, that Jesus rose from the dead. I shared, as much as I could recall from memory, the best arguments I had learned from top biblical scholars. I knew I had him now! How could he deny such a well thought out and eloquently presented "defense" of the Gospel? I was convinced this was going to be a slam dunk. His only response was something to the effect, "Maybe it's true, but I don't know because I wasn't there, and neither were you." How could I respond to that?

All Words, No Power?

So, is this all that we have in our arsenal? A well thought out and reasoned presentation of the Gospel. Is the Gospel only available to those who are "smart" enough to understand and accept its validity? Are we left with reason alone as our sole method of sharing the truth of the Gospel? As a Bible school and seminary student, I focused almost exclusively on the Gospel message (truth) and gave little thought to the Holy Spirit's power in "showing" the truth of the message. I became consumed with learning approaches to sharing the Gospel and defending its truth.

I relied heavily on my training and education as the sole means of winning people to Jesus. I thought, "If I can adequately explain and defend the Gospel message, people will receive Jesus and enter joyfully into His Kingdom." Apart from a reliance on the Holy Spirit's help in pushing people over the edge, I had little thought of the need for His power. The only problem is that the conversation with the homeless guy kept replaying in my mind. I knew there would always be a limit to convincing people of the Gospel's validity through words and arguments alone. In my heart, I knew that some would never believe without proof.

I have since come to accept that the Gospel is most effective when a clear message is presented along with a display of the Holy Spirit's power. His power may be revealed through an inner burning of the heart or as an outward display of God's miraculous power. Regardless, God's purpose is always to reveal His great love. There are countless ways that

God might reveal His love to people and some include miraculous displays of His power. However, most conservatives have primarily emphasized only the non-miraculous displays of the Holy Spirit's power in their Gospel presentations. Charles Pinnock writes:

> *God did not pour the Spirit out for us to exult in it as a private benefit. The purpose was (and is) to empower witnesses to God's Kingdom.*

Often, when we attempt to advance the Kingdom without accessing Kingdom power, we fail to show the fullness of the Gospel message convincingly. After all, who wants to buy a car without first taking it for a test drive? Can we blame people for choosing not to follow a God they can't see, hear, or encounter?

We need the Holy Spirit's power at work, not only convincing hearts of the Gospel's truth, but also displaying its life-changing power in tangible ways. Many have concluded that biblical faith is blind faith, free from any external evidence or support. However, the Gospel, presented by Jesus was constantly and consistently backed by displays of the Holy Spirit's power; why should our approach be any different?

When Jesus sent out the twelve disciples to advance the Kingdom, He gave them illogical instructions with supernatural expectations. Does Jesus expect the same from His followers today? I believe He does. Here are Jesus' instructions to the twelve in Matthew's Gospel:

> *These twelve Jesus sent out with the following instructions: "Do not go among the Gentiles or enter any town of the Samaritans. Go rather to the lost sheep of Israel. As you go, proclaim this message: 'The Kingdom of Heaven has come near.' Heal the sick, raise the dead, cleanse those who have leprosy, drive out demons. Freely you have received; freely give.*   Matthew 10:5-8

Show & Tell

Although a clear proclamation of the Gospel message is certainly necessary to the advancement of the Kingdom of God, Jesus did not limit the Gospel to words alone. In addition to preaching the message of the Father's relentless love, Jesus told His disciples to display the power of the Gospel by "healing the sick, raising the dead, cleansing the lepers, and driving out demons." Wow! Are these realistic expectations for Jesus' followers today? I believe they are.

The proclamation of the Father's love was consistently supported and verified by a display of His power. It was like saying, "God loves you very much, let me show what I mean." James Dunn Comments:

Jesus demonstrated the presence of the Kingdom through acts of the Kingdom. There is no question but that for Jesus… it was not so much a case, 'where I am there is the Kingdom', as 'Where the Spirit is there is the Kingdom'. It was manifestations of the power of God which were the signs of the Kingdom of God.

There is no indication in Scripture that Jesus expected His followers to present a Gospel void of its power. Perhaps this is what Paul meant when he said that some would "have a form of godliness but deny its power" (II Timothy 3:5). What if Jesus' message of the Kingdom had been absent of the miraculous? Would His message have had the same effect without the proof of its validity? It must have been difficult, even for the Pharisees, to deny the reality of the present Kingdom when the evidence of its existence was so clearly on display.

Facing beheading, John the Baptist sent word to Jesus, "Are you the one who was to come, or should we expect someone else?" (Matthew 11:3) Jesus replied:

Go back and report to John what you hear and see: The blind receive sight, the lame walk, those who have leprosy are cured, the deaf hear, the dead are raised, and the good news is preached to the poor.   *Matthew 11:4-5*

Jesus appealed to the miracles He had performed as proof that God was with Him and that John could trust Him despite his bleak circumstances. Jesus reveals that God uses miracles to support the validity of the Gospel message and to show His love for people. This model was mimicked by the disciples and by Jesus' followers throughout every generation of Church history; now its our turn to show God's love and power to our searching generation.

Closing Time At Arby's?

One evening just before Arby's was about to close for the evening, I stopped to grab some food to take home to the girls. As I opened the door to go inside, I heard God say to my spirit, "Ron". I thought to myself, "Ron?" and then heard God gently say, "No, Rob". I paused at the door for a moment and then asked God, what about Rob? Immediately I saw a picture in my mind of a man with crutches with a wrap on his ankle and foot.

After ordering my food, I said to the girl at the cash register, something like, "Is your dad's name Rob, and did he hurt his foot?" I'm not sure how I knew that Rob was someone's dad. I just knew. She said, "no, my dad's name is not Rob." Just then the girl at the drive through window, who overheard our conversation said, "My dad's name is Rob and, yes, he hurt his foot earlier today. I have been worried about him all day."

The two girls looked at me perplexed and asked how I knew this information, so I told them exactly how it happened. Drive-through girl then said something like, "I didn't know God does stuff like that." I said, "I didn't know either, but He does. Can I pray for you and your dad?" We had a short but amazing prayer time and then I said goodbye. I am so thankful that the Gospel is more than just words that we share with others, it's also God's love and power on display.

Sleepy Christians

20

The Spaceship In My Backyard

**The true sign of intelligence
is not knowledge but imagination**
Albert Einstein

I love to stretch the imagination of the young children in my life. Carver and Riley are two siblings in our church with wonderful imaginations. One day I had an idea that I would ask them if they wanted to go for a ride in my spaceship. Riley was not that keen on riding in my spaceship at first, but with a little encouragement from her older brother, she eventually agreed that it was a good idea. It was going pretty well with my story until Carver started asking questions about the specifics of my spaceship.

"Where do you keep it?" he asked. "In the back yard," I responded. "Well, why can't we see it?" "Because it's underground, Geez." I could see his mind spinning as he tried to process how an underground spaceship garage actually works. Then he started in again, "Can you take us for a ride?" "I can't right now," I said, as I tried to come up with a good reason why. "Why not?" Carver asked. "Because the spark plug is broken," I shot back.

For the next few months, most of my conversation with Carver and Riley was filled with discussion about my spaceship. After a while, they began to grow disillusioned with my empty promises to take them for a ride to outer space. They began to doubt my excuses: "It's out of gas. The gastro modulator is acting up again. The flux capacitor is backfiring. I accidently locked the keys in the ship," etc. Eventually, they quit asking me questions, and I assume they have stopped believing in my spaceship altogether. What nerve! I suppose they find it difficult to believe in something they can't see. I believe many people have the same problem with God and His invisible Kingdom.

Evangelism and Younger Generations

The truth is, most people who come to follow Jesus are not "won over" by some Christian vigilante spouting off truths about God on the street. I'm not saying this approach is bad; it just lacks the element of relationship and trust that is helpful in leading people to Jesus.

This is especially true with younger generations who have concluded that most Christians care more about making converts than they do about the actual needs and life situation of the person with whom they are sharing the Gospel. Those from younger generations often view Christians as spiritual headhunters who value numbers more than people. We are often viewed as arrogant, self-righteous, and condescending in our approach to sharing the Gospel.

Studies reveal that most people become followers of Jesus gradually through deep relationships with those they already love and trust. This was Jesus' approach as well. The disciples were transformed gradually by following Him and developing increasingly intimate relationships along the way. In the New Testament, the Gospel was typically presented and backed by a display of the Holy Spirit's power. I believe that God intends for us to use the same method today.

This truth does not diminish the importance of relational intimacy in our approach to sharing Jesus with others. The goal is not simply to give a message or show God's power, but to love people. Love is the power inherent in the Gospel. This love is clearly displayed through Christ's life, death, and resurrection. When those around us encounter the love and power of God working in and through us, they will be moved to consider, for themselves, a relationship with the God we have grown to love.

Extreme and Irrelevant

Many, outside the church, have concluded that Christians are extreme and irrelevant. I believe this is predominantly because we have been too quick to offer judgment and pat theological explanations without offering love or showing the Kingdom's power. We have often been labeled as hateful, arrogant, unloving, and uncaring.

We are considered extreme when we bark out commands without genuine love. We are considered irrelevant when we offer a Gospel void of power and transformation. The answer for those who view Jesus as extreme is an encounter of His love. The answer for those who view Jesus as irrelevant is an encounter with His power. The world is not in need of our judgmental attitudes, our political agenda, or our slick theological explanations. The world is in need of an encounter with God's unconditional love and a clear display of His power.

Extreme Christianity

Some might argue that being labeled as "extreme" could be viewed as a compliment. Something like, "I am radical for Jesus; I am extreme in my faith." However, when outsiders give us the label of extreme, they are not usually paying us a compliment. They typically mean that we are extremely judgmental, extremely arrogant, or extremely self-righteous. Regarding this point, David Kinnaman, author and President of the Barna Group writes:

> *One of the surprising insights from our research is that the growing hostility toward Christians is very much a reflection of what outsiders feel they receive from believers. They say their aggression simply matches the oversized opinions and egos of Christians. One outsider puts it this way: "Most people I meet assume that Christian means very conservative, entrenched in their thinking, anti-gay, anti-choice, angry, violent, illogical, empire builders; they want to convert everyone, and they generally cannot live peacefully with anyone who doesn't believe what they believe."*

Though much of this evaluation may seem unfair, it nevertheless represents the opinions of an increasing number from the younger generations. Fair or not, we are perceived and described in ways that reflect almost the opposite character qualities of Jesus. Showing the true Gospel to younger generations will require a radical change in our approach and a genuine change of heart for those who disagree with us. Somewhere along the way we have become good at theology, but not so good at loving like Jesus loves. Mike Foster writes:

> *Jesus wiped away the tears of the prostitutes, held the hands of the outcasts, and touched the wounds of the sick and the crazy. He hung with the not-so-perfect people of the world and showed them what Christianity was all about. He was never concerned about a person's title, society's name tag, or the sign on their place of work. Porn stars or preachers, gay or straight, Republican or Democrat, it doesn't mean a rip to God. We are all His children, and we are all in need of the stunningly beautiful thing called grace. We know what we need to do, now let's go do it.*

Showing the Gospel as Jesus did will require us to accept and love people right where they are without the continual need to prove that we are right. In doing so, perhaps younger generations will begin to say about us, "Those Christians are extreme in the way that they love." The answer to the claim that Christianity is extreme is a radical encounter of the Father's love. Let's be determined to show it to them.

Irrelevant Christianity

Another conclusion of younger generations is that Christianity is irrelevant to life on Planet Earth. Though many have not given up on God, a growing number have concluded that Christianity in its current forms "just doesn't work." David Kinnaman shares this comment from Eric, age 29: "Christianity seems like an old, broken-down building that I have to drive by every day. I don't even notice it anymore."

Comments like this one reflect a growing sense among young people that the Church that Jesus started is powerless in its ability to transform or to provide a benefit to our daily lives. In his research for the Barna Group, Kinnaman points out that a growing number of churched young people are coming to the same conclusion; Christianity is powerless and irrelevant. He writes:

Most teenagers in America enter adulthood considering themselves to be Christians and saying they have made a personal commitment to Christ. But within a decade, most of these young people will have left the Church and will have placed emotional connection to Christianity on the shelf.

Showing the Gospel to the next generation will require more than reasoned arguments and well-developed sermons. Somehow these young people will have to encounter the present reality of the living God. Jesus consistently displayed the validity of His message through outward displays of Kingdom power. Nothing has changed. Jesus lives in us through the person of the Holy Spirit and is ever eager to reveal himself to a searching generation. The answer to the claim that Christianity is irrelevant is a radical display of the Father's power.

Radical Love and Radical Power

Of course, showing the Gospel begins with meeting the basic human needs of the least, the lost, and the lowest among us. Jesus clearly taught His followers to help the hurting, defend the helpless and speak up for those who have no voice (Matthew 25:35-36). James echoes Jesus by saying:

Religion that God our Father accepts as pure and faultless is this: to look after orphans and widows in their distress and to keep oneself from being polluted by the world.   *James 1:27*

Bringing Heaven to Earth includes displays of Kingdom compassion, caring for the hungry, thirsty, poor, and naked, etc., but it also includes displays of Kingdom power. Coupling Kingdom compassion and Kingdom power together will reveal to the world that God is both loving and capable to meet their needs. To use the language of this chapter, God is Extreme in His love and Relevant in His power.

Some may say, "Wait a minute, didn't Jesus say, 'An evil generation seeks after a sign' (Luke 11:29). Isn't Jesus telling us that signs and wonders are unnecessary, even evil?" I don't think so! It wasn't the desire for a sign that Jesus condemned; it was the rejection of the many signs they had already seen that fueled Jesus' remarks. It was the lack of faith in the midst of such miraculous signs and wonders that Jesus rebuked, not the desire to see a miracle. It would have been rather contradictory for Jesus to imply that the desire to see signs and wonders is evil and yet continue with His routine of healing the sick, opening blind eyes and restoring the lame to wholeness.

As it relates to our supernatural journey, it is vital that we know the Gospel well enough to present it with accuracy and clarity, but it is equally important that we learn to trust God like little children so we can move beyond our human ability and prove the Gospel convincingly. Without displays of the Holy Spirit's power, many will conclude that the Gospel is about as believable as the spaceship in my backyard. Thankfully, the Kingdom of God, unlike my spaceship, is a present and powerful reality among us.

21

Showing The Gospel?

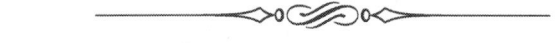

**God loves with a great love the man whose heart is
bursting with a passion for the impossible.**
William Booth

So, I'm gonna guess that some of you are thinking, "But I'm not an extrovert. I get nervous talking to my neighbors, let alone talking to complete strangers I've never met." Thankfully, God didn't reserve the supernatural life for extroverted evangelistic types. The Gospel is best presented within the context of loving, long-term relationships where trust has already been established.

Sure, there will be some who will feel comfortable sharing the Gospel with complete strangers in a public setting, but not everyone is called to share Jesus in this way. The Gospel is not primarily an agenda that we share on special outings, it is a way of life, and we release the presence of God as we walk with Him throughout each day. Let me explain…

Often, when reading through the Gospels, I am confronted by the words of Jesus. I remember reading a passage in the Gospel of Matthew many years ago when I came across some words of Jesus that made no sense to me at the time. Following His instructions to heal the sick, raise the dead, cleanse the lepers, and drive out demons, Jesus sent the disciples out with the following instructions:

Whatever town or village you enter, search there for some worthy person and stay at their house until you leave. As you enter the home, give it your greeting. If the home is deserving, let your peace rest on it; if it is not, let your peace return to you.   Matthew 10:12-13

What did Jesus mean when He said, "If the home is deserving, let your peace rest on it" and if not, "let your peace return?" How do you leave your peace with someone? What does that even look like?

Releasing Peace

Not long ago, a leader in our community approached me about getting together for lunch. I didn't know him well at the time, but I was excited about the possibility of getting to know him better. After a few lunch meetings together, he began to share with me concerning the heavy weight he was carrying at work and how it was affecting life at home as well. He seemed really stressed out; it was evident that he was in great need of God's peace.

I began to ask God to show me how I could release some of the peace in my heart to my friend, you know, like Jesus told the disciples to do. At our next meeting, I sat with my friend and prayed silently for a release of God's peace and love. Toward the end of our time together, my friend sat back in his chair and said something like, "Thank you for meeting with me; I can't describe how much peace I feel when we are together." I almost fell out of my chair.

Releasing Joy

Shortly after this encounter, I received a phone call from a friend from our church who asked if I would come and pray for his mother at the nursing home. Although I had not met his mother, I knew God wanted me to go pray for her. Doris was in her final stages of life and, though her body was shutting down, her mind was sharp, and she was fully alert.

As we talked on the phone, my friend asked if I could encourage his mom and pray for her to receive peace during this time. He said she was very depressed and hadn't smiled or joked for weeks. On the way to the nursing home, I asked God to release the peace and overwhelming joy that I had been experiencing in my time alone with Him. When I entered the room, I found Doris just as my friend had described, depressed with little or no expression on her face.

When I held Doris' hand to pray, a strange thing happened. A small grin appeared on her face. As I began to pray over Doris, she started to shake, and the smile on her face began to grow. As she experienced waves of God's love, her depression was replaced with joy, and her fear was replaced with peace. Doris continued to shake and smile (almost laughing at times) for several minutes as I visited with her.

When I left that day, Doris was no longer afraid of dying. She had experienced a glimpse of what she had to look forward to in the life to come. My friend said that Doris was in a great mood the rest of that evening. When he left, she peacefully went home to be with Jesus.

Releasing Love

Since that day, I have discovered an amazing truth about the Kingdom of God. Whatever we receive from God through impartation, we can also release through His abiding presence within us. Just as we can release peace and joy through His presence, we can also release the transforming power of the Father's love. Here's what I mean…

At a conference I recently attended, God led me to give a fatherly hug to a young man who I had never seen or met before. When I hugged him, I immediately felt the intense love God had for this young man. As we hugged, he began to weep uncontrollably.

I sensed that God was healing something deep within him, so I continued to hug and pray for him for several minutes. After this encounter of God's love, the young man told me that he had never experienced the love of God in this way before and that he had never received pure love from any male figure in his life. I am so thankful for the transforming power of God's love. Whatever God gives us, we can release to others. Freely we receive, freely we give. The Gospel message is not just words, but power. It's not just something we say; it's tangible, it's something we show and give away.

Releasing Power

Years ago, if I were asked to describe the purpose of the local church, I would have responded with something like, "To teach biblical principles, help people apply them to their lives, and teach them how to share these principles with unbelievers (evangelism)." I have since come to believe, even though a primary purpose of the church is to thoroughly understand and communicate the truths of Scripture, speaking the truths of the Gospel is only one part of sharing the Gospel message with the world. Jesus' directive to make disciples was not limited to convincing unbelievers of the Gospel's validity with our well-presented arguments. Paul writes:

> *For I am not ashamed of the Gospel because it is the power of God that brings salvation to everyone who believes: first to the Jew, then to the Gentile.*
>
> *Romans 1:16*

Paul points out that it's the truth of the Gospel, <u>and</u> the power available through it, that convinces skeptics and unbelievers of its validity. For some, including myself, the idea that the Gospel message is intended to be presented together with a display of God's power is a fairly new concept. It is, however, the primary way the Gospel was presented throughout the New Testament.

For many years I struggled with a chronic neck injury I received from playing high school football. On occasion, and especially after long periods of driving, my neck would stiffen, and the pain would increase. There was one small section of my neck that was continuously numb to the touch.

One night, while attending a service in Florida with my family, I was experiencing pain in my neck when an older lady walked past me. She stopped, placed her hand on her neck, and asked me if I was having pain in my neck. I believe God caused her to feel my pain as if it were her own. I said, "Yes." When she placed her hand on my neck and began praying, the pain went away almost instantly. To this day, the pain has not returned even during long car rides or flights. Also, all the feeling has returned to the portion of my neck that had been numb for years.

Evangelism and the Early Church

I am convinced that the primary method of advancing the Kingdom for the early Church, and many Christians throughout Church history, was through a combination of radical love and radical power. Neither Jesus nor the early Christians expected to convert the Roman Empire through the eloquence of words alone. Regarding this fact, Francis MacNutt writes:

> The earliest tradition of the Church taught that the best way to convert pagans was by healing them and casting out evil spirits. This goes back to Jesus' own example, when he sent out the twelve to preach and also commanded them to heal the sick and cast out evil spirits.

Paul's approach to sharing the Gospel, like Jesus' approach, was not reliant on teaching truth alone. Paul was careful to combine a clear Gospel message with a powerful display of the Holy Spirit's power. For example, in writing to the Corinthians he states:

> And so it was with me, brothers and sisters. When I came to you, I did not come with eloquence or human wisdom as I proclaimed to you the testimony about God. For, I resolved to know nothing while I was with you except Jesus Christ and him crucified. I came to you in weakness with great fear and trembling. My message and my preaching were not with wise and persuasive words, but with a demonstration of the Spirit's power, so that your faith might not rest on human wisdom, but on God's power.   I Corinthians 2:1-5

For Paul and the early Christians, the validity of the Gospel message is proven, not by the wisdom or eloquence of human words, but through a clear demonstration of the Holy Spirit's power.

Convincing A Lost World

We have heard missionaries explain that churches in third-world countries rarely thrive without seeing regular displays of the Holy Spirit's power. Spiritualism and witchcraft are blatant in many parts of the world, and the people groups in these countries are quite familiar with the powers of darkness. Unless they witness a display of God's power that exceeds the powers of darkness, they are unlikely to accept and follow Jesus.

Current research has shown that the vast majority of Muslims who are converting to Christianity throughout the world have encountered Jesus through a miraculous dream, vision or supernatural encounter. Ironically, many churches in more "civilized" parts of the world are somewhat skeptical of any such display of the Holy Spirit's power and often grow very large with little or no supernatural evidence of God's presence. However, the apparent lack of transformation and power has contributed to the conclusions that many young people have drawn concerning the irrelevant nature of the western Church today.

Sometimes we become more dependent upon our own ability to convince people of truth than upon God's ability to reveal truth through displays of the Spirit's power. In challenging the Corinthians, Paul writes, "For the Kingdom of God is not a matter of talk but of power" (I Corinthians 4:20). So, let our presentation of the Kingdom be marked by accurate and reasoned communication of the Gospel. But let it also include timely displays of the Holy Spirit's power. Unless the Church relearns the New Testament model of releasing the power of the Kingdom, the effectiveness of the Gospel message will be greatly hindered.

22

Facing My Fears

**It takes courage to move away from the safe place into
the unknown, even when we know that the
safe place offers false safety and the unknown promises
us a saving intimacy with God.**

Henri Nouwen

I remember the day of my 7th-grade football debut. It was the day I had anticipated and diligently prepared for all my life, at least those first twelve years. I had spent many a lunch hour talking myself up. Now it was time to showcase my skills on the field. My entire being, all one hundred and ten pounds of it, shivered with exhilaration as we prepared for battle with our cross-town rivals.

The big day finally arrived, and the atmosphere of McGrath Jr. High School was charged with excitement and energy. At least it felt that way to me. The only problem was, underneath all the talk and outward display of confidence, I was scared to death. I couldn't stop thinking about all the people who would be watching the game. What if I had talked myself up too much? After all, my green beret brother-in-law wasn't there to bail me out this time. What if I forget all the plays? What if I failed miserably? Our biggest fears often become reality. I completed three passes on three attempts that day, all to the other team! So much for my Junior high football debut!

It's no coincidence that the most often repeated command in Scripture is the phrase "Fear Not." God didn't want fear to be a part of our existence on planet Earth. Fear robs us of peace and makes small problems seem big. Fear diverts our attention from God's goodness and distracts us from the possibilities of His Kingdom. Fear steals our hope and fills us with worry and anxiety. Many health professionals argue that fear is a root cause of many physical health problems as well. Fear is harmful to us for many reasons, but perhaps its most harmful effect is hindering the dreams and plans God has for our lives. For many of us, our greatest obstacle to the supernatural journey is fear.

As God began calling our family to a life of adventure with Him, I had moments of fear that threatened to derail my pursuit of a supernatural journey with Him. Let's look at a few of the fears that proved to be my biggest obstacles; maybe one or more of them will be helpful for your supernatural journey as well.

The Fear of Being Deceived

I remember what I used to say to people who came to me and said they had encountered God in a miraculous way. Typically, I would respond with something like, "Be careful. The devil is the deceiver; you can't trust your experiences." I had received this advice somewhere along the way from someone I respected, and it had left me crippled with the fear of being deceived by the enemy or trusting any encounter or experience. After all, how would I know if the experience was from God. It might be the devil trying to deceive me.

When I first became aware of this mental block, God began to show me a very humbling truth. I had been trusting in the devil's ability to deceive me more than the Holy Spirit's ability to guide me into all truth. It occurred to me that I had given the devil far too much credit and God far too little. The reality was, even though I had asked God to guide and direct me, I didn't trust His ability to protect me from the devil's deception. It grieved me when I realized how little I had been trusting God and how much credit I had been giving to the devil in my life.

Many, from my background, shun all experience, believing that openness to subjective revelation may open the door for deception. The Bible, however, points out that deception comes more from pride and arrogance than from openness to an experience of God's presence

(Obadiah 1:3). Provided that we come through the person, Jesus, Scripture encourages, even commands, a pursuit of God's presence. The authors of Scripture never warn us about the possibility of being deceived through a pursuit of God's presence, but they do warn about being closed off to the influence of God's Spirit. Deception is never a danger unless our pursuit of God is coupled with arrogance, pride or a theological distortion of the person of Jesus.

Throughout Scripture, the reality of experiencing God is the logical outcome of living in fellowship with Him. Our faith is bolstered when we experience the truth of who God is and what God does. God is not opposed to His children pursuing His presence. In Fact, the Bible puts forth God's presence as the primary safeguard against deception. We were created to encounter God; therefore, He is vehemently against the pursuit of any other deity or presence apart from Him. Peter said it well in his reply to the Rulers and Elders when he said, "Salvation is found in noone else, for there is no other name under Heaven given to men by which we must be saved" (Acts 4:12).

Christian meditation doesn't seek to empty the mind so another presence may fill it. It involves focusing all of our love and affection on the presence of the one, true God through the Holy Spirit. It has been the failure of the Church in instructing believers to experience the presence of God through meditation, which has opened the door for counterfeit options. Again, this is especially true for younger generations who perceive that there is more to a relationship with God than what is often presented to them. Another quote by Kinnaman is helpful here:

Christianity is perceived as separated from real spiritual vitality and mystery. It seems like a religion of rules and standards. Surprisingly, the Christian faith is seen as disconnected from the supernatural world – a dimension that the vast majority of outsiders believe can be accessed and influenced. Despite outsiders' exposure to church, few say they have experienced God through church.

Throughout Scripture, servants of God longed for and experienced His presence. In fact, it was most often an experience of God's voice or presence that bolstered the faith and resolve of His people.

Fear of Losing Status (Pride)

When God began to move in my life in ways that I had not previously experienced or expected, I knew I would be faced with a major decision. I would have to either deny the reality of what I was experiencing or swallow my pride and admit I had been wrong in what I previously believed about God and His work in the world. At its core, it was a battle with my pride. I was often riddled with thoughts like: "What will others think of me? Will I lose friendships over this? Will my family think I have gone off the deep end? Will people leave our church?"

These were legitimate questions, and somewhat prophetic, but they were all tied to my fear of losing credibility or status. I had to decide both mentally and emotionally if this journey was worth the price. "After all," I reasoned, "God would love me just the same if I decided not to continue on this path." Though I never really thought of myself as a prideful person, the thought of losing friends, status, and respect caused me to stop and question my resolve to move forward in this new journey with God.

God began to show me that I had done a rather masterful job of camouflaging my pride with my theological arguments. Looking back, I can see how I would justify my judgmental attitude toward other believers by overly focusing on minor theological differences. I was puffed up with pride and justified my indifference toward other believers, somehow believing Jesus was pleased with my arrogance and piety.

I could easily identify what was "wrong" with most Christians who differed from my theological position, and though I wouldn't have admitted it at the time, would write them off as less spiritual or theologically inept. I suppose, on some level, I justified my lack of love by villainizing their doctrinal position or, what I perceived as, their less than holy Christian behavior. Ironically, I found it much easier to love those who didn't know God than to love many of my brothers and sisters in Christ; this has become all too common within the Church today.

Bernard of Clairvaux wisely taught that there are four Christian virtues: The first is humility. The second is humility. The third is humility. And, the fourth is humility. Although I didn't seem to have any of these virtues at the time, God began to show me my hypocrisy; and my appreciation began to grow for those who differed from me in their theological leanings. Over the past several years, I have grown in my love and appreciation for those within the body of Christ from differing theological backgrounds.

Though I believe it is important to consider every teaching through the lens of Scripture, I have discovered the wisdom in gaining insight from Christians of various traditions who love Jesus and hold firmly to the Word of God. I also decided that remaining on this journey is worth whatever I need to give up along the way; losing status, reputation, money or position is a small price to pay to gain more of Him.

Fear of Association

Though it may seem petty and trivial, the approach or style of some ministers or ministries prevented me from hearing anything they had to say. Looking back, it was the thought of being associated with these ministries that most turned me off to a pursuit of the miraculous. I was turned off by the show. I assumed, because it's all I had seen, that every supernatural church looked the same way. I reasoned that even if the healing ministry was for today, I couldn't imagine being a part of a church with such pomp and circumstance.

Like others from my evangelical heritage, I struggled with the negative perception I had developed of supernatural ministries. Much of my distaste was based largely on the perception I had developed of televangelists and high-profile healing ministries. As I considered the supernatural journey, I was afraid that I would be identified with much of what I had considered distasteful and unbiblical. I struggled with the endless pleas for money, and the extravagant show that, to me, disqualified their entire ministries.

I know my perceptions of Charismatic Christians were biased, and much of my distaste was unwarranted, but I had developed a negative mental block toward any ministry that hinted of anything supernatural. I was also turned off by the thought that the ministry of healing was reserved only for certain high-profile leaders with less than tactful etiquette and, what appeared to be, a relentless pursuit of wealth.

All this may sound a bit judgmental, and it certainly was, but I am attempting to be transparent about a stumbling block that, I believe, has hindered many Christians from pursuing or even wanting to pursue the supernatural life God desires for them. I share this not to bring shame, but to point out an obstacle that, with a little perspective, can be easily removed from the Church.

I'll admit that much of my offense was directed more at style than doctrine. I couldn't see Jesus making such a show of ministry. Where was the humility? Where was the gentle, loving, unassuming approach that marked Jesus' life? Though I never labeled myself "anti-charismatic," I left little room for experience or the supernatural gifts of the Spirit in my theology. Nevertheless, through our journey, I have learned to lighten up a bit. Not every ministry will look alike and not every minister will have the same approach.

I have discovered that it's not my responsibility to discern the heart and motive of each minister I encounter. I had to admit that what I had quickly judged as arrogance or pride was often just personal confidence and a healthy awareness of God's favor. Regardless, there will always be a variety of ministry styles within the body of Christ, and it's unfair to judge a ministry based on style alone. After all, how boring would it be if each of us were exactly alike in our approach to God?

It Goes Both Ways

Many have similar misperceptions of churches from my background as well. "All Baptists are legalistic and judgmental" or "Baptists are the ones who blow up abortion clinics and picket the funerals of soldiers." There is a tendency to choose the most rotten apple in the bunch and hold it up as an accurate representation of the whole orchard. Unfortunately, this practice happens within all flavors of Christianity, including my own.

I will readily acknowledge that some from our circles have failed to represent Christ well in this area. I am embarrassed by those from my theological heritage who devote entire conferences to speak out against the "doctrinal errors" of fellow believers. Some use the "fear of deception" mantra to justify their lack of love and the blatant anger in their message. I can offer no justification for their behavior. Despite the volume of their voices, their views and heart do not accurately reflect the majority. Please don't allow the bad apples to cause you to write off the entire orchard.

While I'm attempting to be transparent, I would like to share my experience, as an evangelical, in charismatic meetings. I am not sharing to bring shame, but to draw awareness and hopefully encourage more sensitivity. I have occasionally encountered the real or perceived, condescending tone of some from a supernatural background. On occasion, I have felt belittled or judged as less spiritual, or less Holy Spirit filled. Evangelicals are often labeled "spiritually dead, stuffy, stoic," etc.

We are often made to feel like we are less than sons and daughters of God because of an assumed lack of encounter. I realize that some language is unavoidable, but we must go to great lengths not to talk down to others. If we have encountered more of God, it's by His Grace. Our language and approach can often hinder others from hearing what we have to say. We can rejoice in our encounters without making others feel less than Christian.

Asking non-charismatics if they have been baptized in the Holy Spirit or if they believe in the "Full Gospel" can come across condescending and create division. Besides, without a clear understanding of the terminology involved, very little productive communication can take place. We must learn to build bridges rather than walls. Love must triumph over our desire to be right. Encountering God should increase our humility and cause us to honor those who disagree with us. After all, our ultimate goal is not to feel superior to others but to share together in the love of our Heavenly Father.

A Reluctant Title–Sleepy Christians?

I struggled with naming this book "Sleepy Christians" for this reason. I certainly do not want to create a negative feeling or an "us" versus "them" mentality; the heart of this book is to unite, not divide.

As God's children, we are not made up of the "haves" and the "have nots." When it comes to the Kingdom of God, we are all a bit sleepy at times; this is the ongoing battle we all face in the Kingdom. If we are awakened to more of His presence, we rejoice and give Him all the glory. When we approach one another with love and humility, we reveal God's heart for each of His children.

If, as you read this chapter, you found yourself relating to one or more of the fears that hindered my spiritual journey with God, maybe you could spend the next few moments asking God for courage and direction before moving on to the next chapter. Paul reminds us that "God has not given us a Spirit of fear, but of power and of love and of a sound mind" (II Timothy 1:7). I pray that, regardless of the sacrifice or cost, fear will not hinder you from pursuing the fullness of the Christian life available through the power of God's Spirit.

23

These People Are Weird

Christianity should give more offense, more shock to the world than what it is doing.
Dietrich Bonhoeffer

In my opinion, one of the greatest movie series of all time is "The Lord of the Rings" trilogy. These movies, like the book series, are filled with courage, bravery, honor, chivalry, sacrifice and a bit of romance. Of course, the trilogy ends as it should, with the good guys winning and justice prevailing. The good guys unite to form the "Fellowship of the Ring."

The Fellowship sets out to destroy the ring which threatens to bring evil and destruction to Middle Earth. The group is an unlikely union of Hobbits, Dwarves, and Elves, creating an alliance against great odds. Dwarves, Elves, and Hobbits typically keep their distance from one another. Many years of separation, offense, and suspicion prevent them from finding common ground. Together, they discover the great value of their individual parts and learn that they are stronger together than apart. Overcoming years of offense, the Fellowship discovers unity to be their greatest asset in vanquishing evil and establishing peace in Middle Earth. The beauty of the Fellowship of the Ring is seen in the great unity they find in their diversity and in the worth of each member.

What If ?

What if the Church today could, like the Fellowship of the Ring, overcome years of offense and disunity for the sake of God's Kingdom? A huge stumbling block, for the Church in general, is the ease at which we become offended by minor doctrinal differences or spiritual encounters we do not understand; this is supported by the fact that there are an estimated 33,000 Protestant denominations currently present in the world.

Jesus prayed that we would be one, but there is a great lack of unity within the body of Christ today. The supernatural journey requires that we view and approach the body of Christ with love rather than judgment, with a heart for unity rather than division, and with humility rather than pride. C.S. Lewis makes the point clearly when he writes:

There is someone I love, even though I don't approve of what he does. There is someone I accept, though some of his thoughts and actions revolt me. There is someone I forgive, though he hurts the people I love the most. That person is me. There are plenty of things I do that I don't like, but if I can love myself without approving of all I do, I can also love others without approving of all they do. As that truth has been absorbed into my life, it has changed the way I view others.

Offended By What God Does

Offense over God's activity was a huge mental block for me. I would often ask God to show me His love and power, but when I would see it, I would be offended by how it looked. I couldn't get my mind around God doing things that, to me, appeared disorderly, disruptive, illogical, or scary. In hindsight, I was afraid that something similar to what I saw in others would eventually happen to me, and that scared me.

Though I would camouflage my offense in theological language, I was offended that I was witnessing something I could not understand or explain. I was offended at ministry styles that were different than what I was familiar with or didn't understand. I was offended by vocabulary (language) I was unaccustomed to, yet those around me seemed to speak fluently. I was offended in worship services when I would see people fall under the power of God. I assumed they were faking or at least some of them were.

I was offended when people would shake or laugh when touched by the presence of God. Ironically, I was fine when people would cry in God's presence. In my circles, tears were one of the few emotional responses that were generally free from suspicion.

I remember at one point, in the midst of what I felt was utter chaos, being offended at what was happening around me. Despite my poor attitude, I felt God say to my spirit, "I can't take you farther unless you stop being offended." From that point forward, though I still don't fully understand God's methods, I made a commitment not to be offended at what I don't understand. I have learned to heed the words of John Climacus wrote, "We must always find out which way the wind blows, lest we set our sails against it."

I am not implying that every display, in every service, is a genuine move of the Holy Spirit's power, but I have learned that I am ill-equipped to serve as the judge in these situations. With every genuine move of God, there will likely be counterfeits instigated by the devil to bring confusion. I have heard Bill Johnson say, "Bugs are drawn to light. Where there is light, there are bound to be some bugs as well."

Manifestations of the Holy Spirit

I have observed, when touched by the presence of God, a few physical responses are quite common: crying or shaking, falling and laughing, though there are others for sure. These manifestations are very common occurrences throughout both the Old and New Testaments. See for example: (Jeremiah 5:22; Psalm 2:4, 16:11, 126:2; Mark 5:33; Luke 5:8; Acts 2:12; 4:39-31; 16:25-26; I Peter 1:6-8).

Often, these manifestations are so extreme that onlookers mistake them for drunkenness (Acts 2:13-15; Jeremiah 23:9). I would often read about manifestations in Scripture, but then write off all similar manifestations that occur today. From my limited perspective, Scriptural manifestations were mysterious and most present-day manifestations were unbiblical.

Crying, Shaking and Falling

I have observed that sometimes when moved by the intense love of God, people cry or shake. Evangelicals are typically okay with this. The early American Quakers received their name because shaking was a typical manifestation of the Holy Spirit among them. I have also noticed when people encounter the overwhelming peace or glory of God; they often become overwhelmed by God's presence and find it difficult to remain standing.

Some call this being "slain in the Spirit," which doesn't sound like a positive experience at all. I think a more palatable description might be "resting in the Spirit" or being "overcome by the Spirit." Regardless of the language, this is a very common manifestation of the Holy Spirit when He is bringing freedom, refreshing or healing. The Bible is full of references to those who fell prostrate or were unable to remain standing in God's presence.

Laughter

I have always wondered why most movies depict Jesus as if He is always somber and sad when the Bible says that He was filled with joy (Hebrews 1:9; Psalm 45:7). However, I admit, laughter in the church service was difficult for me to understand since I assumed it was just people being disrespectful and inappropriate. When I discovered that laughter was the natural response of a heart set free by the love of God, I began to accept it as a genuine manifestation from Him. Not all laughter reflects God's presence, but true joy will often overflow in holy laughter.

Part of my difficulty with holy laughter came from an unhealthy and unbiblical view of God. I had a difficult time imagining God laughing. "After all," I would reason, "He has a whole world of serious business to attend to." How could God laugh when there is so much pain in the world? Much of my theology concerning God, like others from my background, had originated more from Neo-Platonic philosophy than from Scripture. Unlike the God of Plato, the Bible presents a loving God who is filled with emotions like; sadness, anger, compassion, jealousy and joy.

Despite reports to the contrary, God is perfectly sovereign over everything that's happening on planet Earth. Perhaps God can laugh, in spite of the brokenness in the world, because He is the answer to its pain and has the ultimate power to bring about the restoration of all things. John Piper explains:

Just as our joy is based on the promise that God is strong enough and wise enough to make all things work together for our good, so God's joy is based on that same sovereign control; He makes all things work together for His glory.

The Psalmist writes: "The One enthroned in Heaven laughs" (Psalm 2:4). There is no plan or strategy of the enemy that will succeed in the end. God laughs from Heaven at the futility of everything the enemy attempts against Him.

I now marvel when God frees His children from deep anxiety or depression and fills them with His overflowing joy. Laughter is the only proper response for such a heart set free. Often, holy laughter is simply an overflow of joy that comes from being in God's presence. I now find it a bit odd that I once considered overflowing joy and laughter inappropriate for the church service. After all, if God himself doesn't restrain His laughter and joy, why should we?

One day, while walking through a meadow, John and Charles Wesley found themselves consumed with the joy of the Lord's presence. Though they had intended only to sing a song to the Lord, they found themselves overcome with holy laughter. John writes:

Part of Sunday my brother and I then used to spend walking in the meadows and singing psalms. But one day, just as we were beginning to sing, he burst into loud laughter…and (I) presently after, to laugh as loud as he. Nor could we possibly refrain, though we were ready to tear ourselves into pieces, but we were forced to go home without singing another line.

Why is it so easy to express overwhelming joy when our favorite team scores a touchdown or our child takes her first steps, yet we have difficulty accepting expressions of joy that come from the heart of a good Heavenly Father?

I believe joy is the continual atmosphere of the Godhead. Joy is the constant atmosphere of Heaven. Meister Eckhart comments on this reality by saying:

> ...*the Father laughs at the Son and the Son at the Father, and the laughing brings forth pleasure, and pleasure brings forth joy, and the joy brings forth love.*

Laughter in church makes perfect sense considering that in His presence is "the fullness of joy" (Psalm 16:11). The very atmosphere of Heaven is joy, and this should be reflected in His body, the Church. Sadly, expressions of overflowing joy are often absent from our church experience today.

In some God encounters, individuals experience a combination of two or more of these manifestations. Regardless, the fruit of such encounters is often deep transformation, freedom from bondage, and an increase in holiness.

Maybe you, like me, have struggled with offense over things you don't understand. Maybe you have been turned off by displays, genuine or otherwise, you have witnessed in the body of Christ. Maybe your offense has prevented you from the encounters God intended to bring you closer to Him and more in line with His Kingdom. Now might be a good time to ask God for help with your offense and invite Him to show Himself to you however He may choose, regardless of how it may appear to others.

24

Plugged In

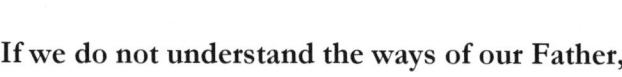

**If we do not understand the ways of our Father,
then it is perfectly understandable why
we are afraid when He is near...**

Leif Hetland

Having had some construction experience through the years, I have become quite familiar with the electrical systems of a new home. There have been occasions, while wiring an outlet, that I forgot to turn off the breaker before going about my business.

Though the wire appears harmless and tame, a sudden ZAP quickly reminds me of the great power that's flowing through the circuit. My body responds in unusual ways to the power it encounters. The presence of God's Spirit is infinitely more powerful than any electrical circuit we will encounter; often our bodies respond to Him in odd ways.

There are many opinions concerning the question of why manifestations so commonly accompany the presence of the Holy Spirit. Some have suggested that God uses manifestations to break pride, root out selfishness, or highlight vain ambition. Others have reasoned that they are simply an indication that God is healing some form of brokenness or pain within us.

From my experience, God uses these encounters to awaken us to His presence and to move us toward greater transformation or spiritual breakthrough. God relentlessly pursues us. Manifestations of his presence only reveal that He is near.

Of course, it's not the manifestation itself that brings about transformation, but the presence of God. On a practical level, manifestations might be viewed as the natural response of the human body to the glory of God's powerful presence.

Revival and Manifestations

Within virtually every revival throughout the history of the Church, manifestations of the Holy Spirit have been present. In fact, it seems the greater the revival, the greater the number and intensity of these manifestations. John Wesley, the founder of Methodism, described the manifestations in one service at their church by saying:

> *People dropped on every side as thunderstruck as they fell to the ground, others with convulsions exceeding all description and many reported seeing visions. Some shook like a cloth in the wind, others roared and screamed or fell down with involuntary laughter.*

Concerning these manifestations, Wesley states:

> *I trust we shall all suffer God to carry on His own work in the way that pleases Him.*

Jonathan Edwards, the great revivalist and President of Princeton University, often spoke of the manifestations that regularly occurred in his church services. As revival began to spread through his congregation, Edwards described the many "odd" manifestations that took place by writing:

> *It was common to see outcries, fainting, convulsions with distress and joy. Some were so affected that their bodies were overcome, so they stayed all night in the church.*

Manifestations were common in his church among all age groups.

Concerning the move of God among the young people in his congregation, Edwards adds:

Many young people appeared to be overcome with the greatness of divine things and many others at the same time were overcome with distress about their sinful state so that the whole room was full of nothing but outcries, fainting and such like and many were overpowered and continued there for some hours.

One thing that struck me about these "odd" manifestations was that those who were experiencing them were finding freedom from bondage that, from my observation, was far less common in my spiritual heritage. Charles Wesley warned his listeners to come down from the trees before he began to speak because some had been falling from them when the Holy Spirit came upon them.

Jonathan Edwards was heavily criticized for the shaking, crying and shrieking that occurred in his church services. The great revivals were criticized or rejected by many of the religious people of their day because of manifestations they did not understand. When addressing questions concerning the validity of these manifestations Edwards writes:

The influence persons are under is not to be judged of one way or other by such effects on the body; and the reason is because the Scripture nowhere gives us any such rule. We cannot conclude that persons are under the influence of the true Spirit because we see such effects upon their bodies, because this is not given as a mark of the true Spirit; nor on the other hand, have we any reason to conclude from any such outward appearances, that persons are not under the influence of the Spirit of God, because there is no rule of Scripture given us to judge of spirits by, that does either expressly or indirectly exclude such effects on the body, nor does reason exclude them.

Edwards' went on to write a treatise in defense of manifestations which has served as a foundational resource on the topic. In his writing, Edwards suggests that the genuine nature of manifestations can only be determined by the fruit they produce. He then pointed to the transformation and positive affect that was taking place among those who were experiencing these manifestations as evidence that they were birthed of God's Spirit.

I am not suggesting that all manifestations are born of God. But when God's presence is active among His people there is often a considerable effect on the human body. Also, some of the greatest transformation I have witnessed as a pastor has occurred in people who have encountered the radical love of God. Sometimes, but not always, these great outpourings of love are accompanied by some form of manifestation.

Although manifestations aren't present every time God works in a person's life, they are fairly common and shouldn't be viewed with suspicion simply because we are uncomfortable with the way they appear. They are simply to be understood as the phenomenon of the body's response to the actual tangible presence of God. Trying to overanalyze or predict how the Holy Spirit will affect a given person is a fruitless exercise. Richard Rohr comments:

We don't know how to dogmatize or control the wind, water or doves alighting from the sky. Such deliberate and daring metaphors for God should keep us rightly humble in all our knowing, predicting and explaining.

Though it is difficult to fully understand how or why the human body is affected by the presence of God, it's evident from Scripture and Church history that manifestations of the Holy Spirit are part of the normal Christian life. Wherever and whenever the Holy Spirit moves in power, there will likely be some external evidence of His presence among His people. Since we want Him to move in and through us, we will also need to embrace the effects of His presence on our natural bodies as well.

Of course, we are not in pursuit of a manifestation; we are in pursuit of God. This should be self-evident, but often the lines become blurred. In our pursuit of more of His presence, may we overcome our offense at the things we cannot understand and allow God to reveal himself however He may choose.

25

When God Is A No Show

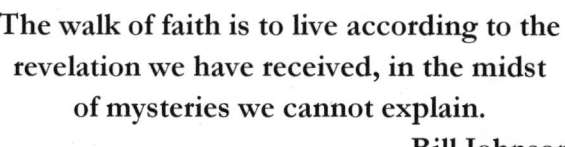

**The walk of faith is to live according to the
revelation we have received, in the midst
of mysteries we cannot explain.**

Bill Johnson

Earlier, I shared a story about a beautiful little girl whose hearing was restored through the prayers of ordinary people. We all celebrated the victory and rejoiced with this wonderful family. We felt God's goodness and declared it loudly. Not long after this miraculous event, we were informed that the little girl's brother was diagnosed with Leukemia. On several occasions, we surrounded him and prayed for his healing, fully believing for his recovery.

When things looked bad, we united in prayer and asked God to bring Heaven to Earth once again. When our little hero began to improve, we celebrated and rejoiced over his progress. After battling for what seemed like eternity, this precious little boy went home to be with Jesus. We were overcome with grief for this young family and struggled to make sense of the lack of breakthrough.

More recently, my mom was diagnosed with a very aggressive form of cancer. Within a short time, cancer had spread throughout her body. Once again, we fervently prayed for her healing. In less than three months after mom was diagnosed, she passed away. Our church family mourned once again over the loss of another heartbreaking battle.

In our supernatural journey with God, there will certainly be great moments of victory when the enemy's plans fail, and Heaven comes to Earth through our prayers. However, there will likely also be times of defeat when we become frustrated, confused and disillusioned when our prayers remain unanswered. If we are not careful, we may find ourselves offended by our questions regarding God's inactivity.

Does God Play Favorites?

Although God's unexplainable activity was a large stumbling block in my journey, it was actually His inactivity that proved to be the largest obstacle in my pursuit of Him. In particular, it was the concept of supernatural healing that most offended my conservative mindset. I found it difficult to accept that some were healed, and others were not. "After all," I reasoned, "was God playing favorites by picking and choosing who He would heal and who He would allow to remain sick or die?"

I was also offended by those who claimed that they had received healing, but didn't, in my opinion, appear to deserve it. Why would God heal unworthy people yet allow my dad to die from heart disease? The topic of healing had become very personal to me. Was God unloving or unfair? I wasn't willing to accept either of these conclusions. So, from my perspective, it only made logical sense to conclude that God doesn't heal today or that His healing activity is rare and mysterious.

Though I didn't realize it at the time, this solution inadvertently makes God responsible for sickness, death and dying. If not directly, God's inactivity forces us to conclude that He is, at least indirectly, responsible. After all, we prayed, and nothing happened, therefore, God must have said no! As a pastor, I remember trying to bring comfort to young parents who had lost a baby by saying something like, "God wanted the baby to be with Him. God must have decided to take His little angel home." Though well intentioned, I have come to believe that statements like these do not reflect the truths found in Scripture regarding healing and God's will.

Does God Always Get His Way?

Some suggest that because God is sovereign, He always gets His way; His will is always done. Though this view of God's sovereignty is common among believers today, it's actually more Platonic than Biblical. Scripture presents a God who is in control but who chooses not to control everything. Plato, Aristotle and others taught that God's sovereignty means that all sickness and disease which end in death must also fall within His sovereign plan. However, do the Scriptures teach that God always gets His way or that His will is always done on Earth? Can we conclude that God's sovereignty proves that His will is always accomplished perfectly on Earth? I don't think so...

If so, why did Jesus ask us to pray... "Your Kingdom come, your will be done, on Earth as it is in Heaven" (Matthew 6:10). Certainly, Jesus would not have us pray daily for a reality that already exists. Peter writes, "He is patient with you, not wanting anyone to perish, but everyone come to repentance" (II Peter 3:9). Do some perish without accepting Jesus? Yes, unfortunately, many do. And, when they do, God's will is not accomplished on Earth. Bill Johnson eloquently writes:

> *God's ability to use bad things for His glory has caused some to think that He is the author of those bad things. This belief usually gets swept under the mysterious carpet called God's sovereignty. While I love and delight in the wonder of our sovereign God, I am grieved at how much in our lives is inconsistent with Jesus' life, yet gets labeled as God's mysterious will.*

The idea that God wills everything that occurs goes beyond the limits of a biblical representation of God's sovereignty. Are we willing to include the fall of humanity, the existence of evil, the Holocaust, ethnic cleansing, world wars, etc., within the canopy of God's sovereign will, or even His permissive will? Can we reconcile God's love with His responsibility for such atrocities? It's best to admit that perhaps the Church has often mis-defined God's sovereignty based on the extra-biblical Greek philosophies which influenced many early Christian thinkers.

I have come to believe that it's God's will for all to be healed just as it is His will that all be saved. The New Testament word for salvation is *sozo*. The word refers to salvation from sin, sickness and spiritual bondage. The reality that many remain lame, sick or in bondage is more of a reflection on the sleepy nature of the Church than on God's inactivity. We simply have yet to fulfill our God-given destiny of bringing Heaven to Earth. We should never allow the lack in our lives to determine our theology of healing. Instead, our lack should create a longing for everything Jesus paid for on the cross.

In His sovereignty, God has seen fit to subject himself, at least to some degree, to the free choices of men. Ironically, the Creator of the Universe makes Himself vulnerable to those He created in His own image. We may freely choose to follow and love Him, or we may choose to reject and despise Him. Regardless of our theological leanings, it is difficult to conclude from Scripture that God's sovereignty proves that His will is always accomplished on Earth.

Jesus and Healing

The New Testament is filled with the tension of God's inactivity. Not everyone who was lame, sick, or diseased was healed by Jesus when He walked on the Earth. When Jesus healed the man at the pool of Siloam, there were many others at the pool who remained lame or sick (John 5:1-15). However, Jesus never turned anyone away who came for deliverance or healing. He never said, "Sorry, there is too much sin in your life," or "It's not God's will for you to be healed at this time."

Jesus didn't assume that God has a mysterious purpose for sickness, or that God brings calamity upon His children to build greater character in their lives. In Scripture, sickness and disease are not viewed as a blessing in disguise. Although God often used sickness and disease to reveal His goodness, Jesus never hinted that God gives sickness and disease to His children.

Some have suggested that Paul's thorn in the flesh (II Corinthians 12:7-10) was a disease, a sickness, or a physical ailment that God gave to Paul in order to keep him humble. The context of the passage makes it much more likely that this "thorn" was a demonic messenger, or an antagonistic adversary sent by Satan to harass Paul. The context identifies Paul's infirmities as imprisonments, shipwrecks, stonings, beatings, etc. Though he was weak from persecution, there is no mention of sickness, disease or physical ailment. Whenever "thorns" are mentioned elsewhere in Scripture, they are adversaries, not sickness or disease. (Numbers 33:55; Joshua 23:13; Judges 2:3) Paul was not praying in this passage for God to remove sickness or disease but persecution.

God's will in regard to healing is clearly on display in the life of Jesus. Peter proclaims:

You know what has happened throughout Judea, beginning in Galilee after the baptism that John preached. How God anointed Jesus of Nazareth with the Holy Spirit and power, and how he went around doing good and healing all who were under the power of the devil because God was with him   Acts 10:38

All who came to Jesus for healing received and all who came seeking freedom from bondage were set free. In Nazareth, where few were healed, Jesus explained that the villain was their "lack of belief" rather than God's unwillingness to heal.

To Jesus, it was never a question of God's willingness to heal since the Father is always willing. It is His desire to give His children full access to the things of the Kingdom. Jesus said, "Do not be afraid, little flock, for your Father has been pleased to give you the Kingdom" (Luke 12:32). The Kingdom includes everything that Jesus paid for on the cross, our freedom from both the power and penalty of sin.

The theological view that sickness and disease are tools that God routinely uses to train or discipline His children is difficult to support from Scripture. Instead, we see Jesus constantly going from place to place doing good, healing the sick, bringing sight to the blind, making the lame to walk and rescuing all those who were in bondage to the devil. God wants to use us in similar ways.

If we pray and healing does not occur, it's not helpful to conclude that God's will has been done in such instances. It is difficult to find biblical support for such a theology. So what then is actually taking place when God appears to be a no show?

Sleepy Christians

When God Is A No Show

26

A Map Or A War?

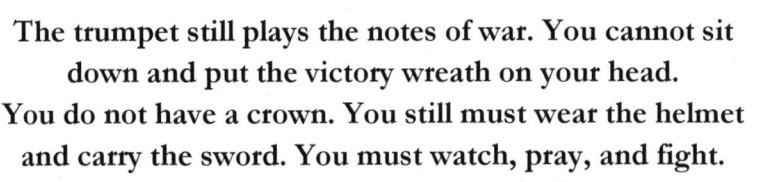

**The trumpet still plays the notes of war. You cannot sit
down and put the victory wreath on your head.
You do not have a crown. You still must wear the helmet
and carry the sword. You must watch, pray, and fight.
Expect your last battle to be the most difficult, for the
enemy's fiercest charge is reserved for the end of the day.**
Charles Spurgeon

When a child imagines him or herself fighting off evil villains, ruling over vast kingdoms, or defending innocent townspeople from fire breathing dragons, maybe they are not as out of touch with reality as we might think.

Could it be that part of what Jesus meant when He said "Do not hinder the little children from coming to me, for such is the Kingdom of Heaven" is that children, in addition to their humility and childlike faith, tend to understand and accept the realities of God's Kingdom better than most adults?

Maybe adults, more than children, have lost sight of their destiny as joint heirs with Jesus in the fight against injustice and the vanquishing of evil from His good universe. Maybe part of becoming more childlike is growing in our understanding of God's call to increasingly participate in the spiritual war taking place all around us.

After all, doesn't the Bible present a cosmic picture of good versus evil where good wins and justice prevails? Doesn't Jesus consistently remind us of a devil who, as our adversary, comes to kill, steal and destroy? Paul writes:

Finally, be strong in the Lord and his mighty power. Put on the full armor of God, so that you can take your stand against the devil's schemes. For our struggle is not against flesh and blood, but against the rulers, against the authorities, against the powers of this dark world and the spiritual forces of evil in the heavenly realms.   *Ephesians 6:10-12*

Jesus consistently spoke of a spiritual battle that has existed between the devil and God's creation since the fall. He pointed to this spiritual battle as the nemesis to the supernatural life of the Kingdom. Sickness, disease, bondage and death, according to Scripture, have always been the work of the devil.

A Map or a War?

The worldview of the early Church was that of a spiritual war between the devil and God's most prized creation, us. In the early Church, death, disease, and spiritual bondage were viewed through this lens. This worldview went somewhat unchallenged for the first few centuries of the Church until some prominent Greek philosophers came to follow Jesus. The Christian worldview began shifting, in part, because of the influence of Greek philosophy upon many prominent Christian leaders in the early Church.

The teachings of Plato and Aristotle concerning God's complete immutability, timelessness, impassability, and transcendence were adopted by some of the early Church Fathers, and later, by Augustine in the 5th century. Augustine, who was influenced heavily by the Hellenistic philosophies of his youth, presented the Church with a new lens through which to view the world.

In his map view, Augustine suggested that good, evil, death, and disease must be interpreted through the lens of God's sovereign will. The warfare lens was replaced with the map lens. Under the map lens, it became increasingly taught that anything which occurs within God's creation occurs because God, our sovereign Father, has willed it to be so. For the first time, on a wide scale, Christians began to place death, sickness, disease and the existence of evil within the category of God's sovereign will.

I'm not trying to throw Augustine under the bus or take away from the many great contributions he has made to the Church, but his definition of sovereignty sounds more like Plato than Jesus. To conclude that God always gets his way or that His will is always accomplished on Earth is to give God credit for much of what the devil does. Augustine, like many of the Greek Christian philosophers and theologians of his day, interpreted the Scriptures through a Hellenistic lens; this is to be expected since they lived and learned in a Greek world.

Though they had a deep commitment to the Word of God, they read and interpreted Scripture with Greek eyes. Augustine's adoption of Greek philosophical ideas coupled with his wide influence within the Church has left many with a distorted understanding of God's sovereign will. His Neo-platonic philosophies, later adopted by many prominent Christian thinkers, have led, in part, to a reduced expectancy for divine healing within the Church and a misunderstanding of God's work in the world today. I believe John Sanders is correct in writing:

> *For the history of the biblical classical synthesis there is no more significant Western theologian than Augustine. He was deeply influenced by the Neo-Platonism he learned from Plotinus, which, even in his mature years, he used to interpret the Bible.*

The reality of evil, including sickness and disease, are best viewed from the vantage point of the enemy's attack against the children of God rather than a reflection on God's choice. We are at war; we have an enemy. The devil, not God, is to blame for the brokenness, bondage, sickness, disease and death in the world. Charles Pinnock writes:

> *Jesus announces that God's rule is near but not yet in full effect. At present, God's will is resisted by powers of darkness, but the day will come when his*

will shall triumph. At present, evil is mounting a challenge to God's rule with considerable effect. The powers of darkness put up stiff resistance and to a degree block God's plans; that is, they can restrict God's ability to respond to a given crisis. Hence Paul says that the Spirit groans and waits with us for the final redemption (Romans 8:23). God's ability to turn things around is circumscribed in ways we cannot understand, yet this is more than countered by the hope of the coming Kingdom. Evil may have its day, but it will not finally triumph.

Why Do Bad Things Happen?

When asked the question, "Why do bad things happen?" The early Church would have responded in unison, "There is a devil, we are at war. The enemy comes to kill, steal, and destroy." Today, more often than not, Christians are responding with something like, "We don't understand it, it's a mystery, but it's all part of God's sovereign plan." When a soldier is lost in battle, rarely do we question the source of the loss; the loss comes at the hands of the enemy. Today we often claim that the shots are being fired within our own camp. This quote from Bill Johnson sums it up quite well:

God is good. The devil is bad. Health and healing are good. Sickness and disease are bad. It's not complicated.

Our supernatural journey with God will require us to change our thinking concerning His goodness. We must also stop being offended at God for, what we perceive to be, His inactivity. We must reevaluate our thoughts concerning His sovereignty. God's omnipotence and sovereignty do not prove that nothing can go contrary to His will; many of our sinful choices and actions are contrary to His will yet God is still sovereign.

When tragedy strikes or evil occurs, we must remember that He is for us, not against us. He does not bring calamity upon His children to punish them or to teach them a lesson. He is a good Father, and He loves to give good gifts to His children. However, we do have an enemy; we are at war. It is the enemy who comes to kill, steal and destroy. Jesus came to free us from the devil's tyranny and to give us abundant life.

Though God has created our world, He does not currently control every aspect of His creation. Through the fall, the world became subject to futility, meaning that all of creation was affected in some way by Adam and Eve's choice. (Romans 8:20-22) The natural world is subject to natural laws as well. Just as we cannot blame every natural disaster on God's sovereign hand, we cannot point to God as the originator and distributor of sickness and disease. Bad things happen in a world where God is in control but has chosen to not control every aspect of His creation.

Though we cannot fully understand this side of eternity, why some are healed, and others are not, the tension remains unresolved by the false assumption that God no longer heals today or that God, in His sovereignty, brings sickness and disease upon His children. This conclusion violates Scripture and the clear testimony of history. "Jesus Christ is the same yesterday and today and forever" (Hebrews 13:8). He is and forever will be "Jehovah Rapha," the God who heals. Though there is mystery, the answers seem to be wrapped up in the choices that we make, the natural laws of our created universe which is now subject to futility and our willingness to participate in the present Kingdom that Jesus has made available to us.

Perhaps you, like me, have been offended by the unanswered prayers in your life. Maybe your theological training has prompted you to conclude that every bad thing that has happened in your life is the result of God's sovereign choice. For many, it's difficult to reconcile God's love with the reality of their circumstances. Unfortunately, those walking through pain rarely find comfort in hearing that God has allowed their pain for their own good.

It's time to stop making excuses for God. A biblical understanding of healing and God's heart will alleviate our need to do so. God is inviting us to think of His goodness as a continual and relentless reality, regardless of our circumstances? Have you stopped to consider the implications of spiritual warfare on death, disease, and spiritual bondage in our world? Maybe the reason God doesn't always get His way has less to do with His inactivity and more to do with ours.

27

Theological Tunnel Vision

Before we do anything else, we must become convinced of our selective deafness to a great deal we should be listening to.
Benedict J. Groeschel

When my second, oldest daughter, Emma, was just a toddler, my wife went away for the evening placing Emma fully in my care. Normally this wouldn't have been a problem, but on this occasion, I had a lot of work to complete, and I'm not the world's greatest multi-tasker. I assured Tara that Emma was in good hands and that she could relax and enjoy her evening out.

Everything started out great. I had Emma fairly content in her bouncy seat while I was making progress on my work. She started to get a little fussy, so I looked around for something to capture her attention. Glancing over my desk, I spotted a blue highlighter and thought it would be a good option to occupy her. I was completely engrossed in my work when I realized that Emma had been uncharacteristically quiet.

When I paused to look down at her, I noticed Emma had managed to work the top off of the highlighter and was using it as her pacifier. Her face and hands were completely covered in blue. Looking in her mouth, it appeared as if she had completely sucked my highlighter dry. Frantically searching, I found the small lettering on the highlighter which read: "non-toxic." I breathed a sigh of relief. I spent the next couple of hours scrubbing Emma's face, hands, and tongue while giving her a lot of juice to wash away the evidence. When Tara got home and asked how everything went, I said, "Fine." I had dodged a bullet, or so I thought. The next day, while changing Emma's diaper, Tara discovered what goes in blue, oddly comes out bluish-green.

How does this story relate to our supernatural journey with God? I have found, when it comes to our pursuit of truth, we can have theological tunnel vision that prevents us from seeing the bigger picture of God's plan for His Kingdom. We can be so focused on our individualized work in the Kingdom that we lose sight of what is taking place outside of our own little world.

One problem with the Church today is that Christians tend to do life in their own camps and rarely rub shoulders with others outside of their immediate circles. The next section looks at a few areas where Christians have often experienced "theological tunnel vision." Who knows, maybe God will "highlight" something that will awaken you to His supernatural plans for your life. Again, if you'd rather get punched in the face than talk theology, then feel free to jump ahead.

Rapture Theology

Over the past one hundred years, a theology of "escapism" has developed that, to some extent, is inconsistent with the heart and teaching of Jesus. This view, also known as Rapture theology, is based largely on I Thessalonians 4:17 and the book of Revelation. Popularized by the highly successful book and movie series, "Left Behind," this view has gradually become the primary teaching in western theology concerning the events of the end-times.

Though rapture theology has been a highly accepted view in America over the past fifty years, it has failed to gain wide support around the world. Rapture theology is a fairly recent doctrine that some theologians have labeled "the American Phenomenon." I am not here attempting to debate the reality or non-reality of a future rapture, I simply want to highlight a theological mindset that often surrounds this view that has hindered the church from embracing the spiritual power that Jesus promised to His followers.

Painting broad strokes, I will attempt to outline this view in a few short sentences. Ready? As we draw near to the end of days, the world will increasingly become a wicked place ruled and dominated by the devil and his entourage. The Church of Jesus will slowly become a lukewarm and ineffective witness to the world. Wars, earthquakes, famine and pestilence will dominate the globe as food becomes scarce and the anti-Christ gains greater control of world governments. The Church will continue to weaken and decline as the devil pours out his wrath on those who refuse to submit to his rule.

As the end approaches, the Church will become predominately apostate and ineffectual in its witness to the world and its ability to slow the advance of evil upon the Earth. The anti-Christ will gain control and power of the world system and unleash a terrible attack on those who continue to hold an allegiance to the Lamb. Before (Pre-Trib), during (Mid-Trib) or after (Post-Trib), the height of this great time of tribulation, Jesus will return to "snatch away" or "rapture" those who have remained faithful to Him.

The second coming, usually viewed as a separate event, will follow this time of great distress. Jesus will defeat the devil and his entourage and bring swift justice upon the Earth. He will establish His Kingdom, there will be a judgment of the righteous and unrighteous, the devil will be defeated and judged, and we will live forever, on Earth (or in Heaven), with Jesus as our reigning King. I realize that I have painted broad strokes and that there is a world of variation within this theological system. My intention is only to give a general outline so we can discuss how rapture theology has somewhat impacted our supernatural expectation.

Tunnel Vision on the Power of Evil

Though a full discussion of Eschatology (doctrine of last things) is beyond the scope of this book, there are two assumptions, common within Rapture theology, that seem to run contrary to the clear teaching of Scripture; I will approach them in the form of questions. First, does the Bible teach that the Church Jesus established and commissioned will become apostate and powerless against the rise of evil upon the Earth? I do not believe that it does. Second, does the Bible teach that the Kingdom of God is, for the most part, a future destination awaiting Jesus' return to Earth or our future escape to Heaven? I don't think so.

A fundamental problem with Rapture theology, as it relates to our supernatural journey with God, is that it portrays the Church as a weak and powerless force against the rise of evil upon the Earth. Due to the lukewarm condition of God's people during the end-times, the only real hope for the Church is to avoid the incessant rise of evil by escaping it before things get really bad during the tribulation period. Though the New Testament teaches that there will be an increase of evil on the Earth during the end-times, it does not follow that the Church will be lukewarm or powerless against this rise of evil upon the Earth.

The New Testament paints an entirely different picture of the end-time Church. Although the devil and his entourage will increase their attack on the righteous, their efforts will ultimately fail and prove no match for the presence and power of God working through His Church. The effect of emphasizing the rise of evil on the Earth, to the exclusion of the Church's ability to overcome evil, has caused many believers to accept a timid or defensive attitude toward the forces of darkness and to lose sight of their calling to bring God's redemptive plan to fruition.

Some imagine an end-time Church that is wrought with sin and apostasy. There is the suggestion that Jesus must return quickly before every believer abandons the faith altogether. However, this view of the end-time Church doesn't fit the description of the Bride in the book of Revelation:

Let us rejoice and be glad and give Him glory! For the wedding of the Lamb has come, and his bride has made herself ready.   Revelation 19:7

Jesus is not returning for an apostate Bride (Church) with a filthy wedding dress. Bill Johnson once commented on this passage by saying that Jesus isn't coming back for a "dirty, unfaithful wreck of a woman, but for a spotless Bride who has made herself ready." The end-time Church, through the transforming power of the Holy Spirit, will become increasingly holy, filled with power and overwhelmingly effective at bringing God's Kingdom to Earth.

Tunnel Vision on Darkness

I sometimes have fellow Jesus followers approach me in fear of the impending "doom" we face as a nation or Church. I have a difficult time blaming them for their fear since we are constantly bombarded with doomsday reports from the media. The focus always seems to be the strife in the Middle East, the terrorism that has come to America, or the increase of crime and racism in our cities. Every societal event is viewed as the fulfillment of prophecy and cause for major alarm; "The end is surely coming soon."

The devil's agenda is to overwhelm us with his activity on planet Earth and cause us to live in fear rather than faith. I've heard stories, even recently, of Christians who are stockpiling food, water, and supplies in preparation for some imminent trial or tribulation that is sure to come. Does God intend for His children to live defensively in fear of the devil's plans? I don't think so!

I am not suggesting that hardships won't come or that we should just bury our heads in the sand and ignore reality. However, Jesus never hinted that we should live in fear of the future or of the enemy's plans. If our focus is on the enemy, we lose our focus on Jesus and begin to take a defensive posture toward evil and darkness.

Although Jesus acknowledged the devil's evil intent, His emphasis was never on the inferior powers of darkness, but on the overwhelming power of the light. Jesus constantly reminded His followers of the power of His Church and its influence in advancing His Kingdom on Earth. Michael Maiden addresses this by writing:

> *We have believed a theology that says the enemy will overwhelm the Church and Christians will barely escape at the last moment. And yet, is it not curious that the Bible speaks of the last days as the "Day of the Lord" rather than the "day of the devil?"*

The view of a timid and powerless end-time Church is not found in the

New Testament or the teachings of Jesus. Jesus clearly stated His intention in establishing the Church when He said, "Upon this Rock, I will build my Church and the gates of hell will not stand against it" (Matthew 16:18). He presented a vivid picture of His Church on the offensive against the strongholds of the enemy with no thought of defeat or need for fleeing. N.T. Wright clearly states Jesus' intention for His Church on Earth when he writes:

Jesus' resurrection is the beginning of God's new project not to snatch people away from Earth to Heaven, but to colonize Earth with the life of Heaven. That, after all, is what the Lord's Prayer is all about.

There is no mention in Jesus' teaching of a feeble, unholy, intimidated group of powerless believers cowering together awaiting a heavenly rescue. On the contrary, the picture presented in Scripture is of a dynamic gathering of Spirit-empowered Kingdom fighters storming the gates of hell and preparing the way for the glorious coming of Jesus, the King. In fact, Jesus himself described the advancement of the Kingdom of God on Earth with less passivity than is often presented within the Church today. He said, "…until today the Kingdom is advancing and the righteous take it by force" (Matthew 11:12). Yeah!

God did not intend for His followers to live in fear of the devil or the rise of evil in the world. We have not been given the mandate to stockpile and hide out until Jesus returns. Ours is not a call to "hold the fort" and wait for rescue, but to storm the gates of hell through the power of the Holy Spirit who lives within each of us.

Could it be that Satan has used this distraction to prevent God's children from living out their mandate of advancing the Kingdom with expectation, hope, and joy? Could it be, even though there is an increase of evil rising upon the Earth, we, the Church, really are equipped to be victorious in destroying the works of the devil and overcoming his evil plans? Absolutely!

God is so big and His decrees so definite that when He says, "The gates of hell will not prevail" against the power of the Church, He has the ability to bring it to pass. Contrary to popular opinion, the Church

Jesus founded is not destined for failure. The Church will not become increasingly powerless and ineffective in witness and power. God is awakening His Church and equipping her for battle, a battle that she will decisively win.

Perhaps you too have been overly focused on the powers of darkness and have underestimated the power of the Light. Maybe there have been moments when you have been overcome with fear as you consider the future of our country, your family, or the world. It's time to look at the future through the eyes of Jesus and stop living in fear of the devil. "What, then, shall we say in response to these things, if God is for us, who can be against us" (Romans 8:31)?

Tunnel Vision on the Future, Other Worldly Kingdom

There has also been a theological tendency in the Church to teach that the Kingdom of God is primarily a future Kingdom that is far removed from planet Earth. The word *basileia* appears throughout the New Testament and is typically a reference to "the reign or dominion" of God. The Kingdom becomes a reality whenever and wherever God's presence brings justice, righteousness, and transformation.

Although the future reality of God's Kingdom is central to the Christian hope, it is not the only hope for God's people. The reign of God is firmly established in Heaven and is being established on Earth through men and women who give themselves to Jesus and commit to "seek first His Kingdom" (Matt 6:33).

The consummation of the Kingdom is clearly presented in the book of Revelation when John writes, "The Kingdoms of the world have become the Kingdom of our Lord and of his Messiah, and He will reign forever and ever" (Rev 11:15). At that time, God's reign will be firmly established "on Earth as it is in Heaven." Jesus taught us to pray and live daily with this end in mind.

The topic of the Kingdom is popular among Christians today. However, much of the conversation centers upon a future Heavenly Kingdom that we will all enter someday when we die or that Jesus will establish upon His return to Earth. The idea that the Kingdom of God is other worldly with little earthly relevance is not a biblical concept. This idea is another carryover from Greek philosophy.

The biblical teaching concerning the Kingdom is that it is present and readily accessible within our space and time. Though our future hope of being in the fullness of God's presence is a real and exciting part of God's plan, there is a present reality of the Kingdom that seems to get more press from Jesus.

A Present Kingdom Hope

From my perspective, the Church, in large part, has given up on a present Kingdom hope here on Earth. Why? Theologians discuss this topic using the terminology "the already but not yet," meaning the Kingdom of God is present (already), but the Kingdom of God is also future (not yet). Though the terminology is useful, some theologians emphasize the "not yet" dimension of the Kingdom to a far greater degree than the "already."

For the most part, theologians agree that the Kingdom was initiated with Jesus' first coming. However, if you were to ask most Western Christians about their "hope in Christ," they would likely begin a discussion about Heaven and their expectation of leaving this Earth to go there one day. Again, Maiden comments:

> The majority of evangelical Christians in America believe that the Earth and the nations are so polluted, corrupted by evil and devastated by sin, that change for the good is hopeless. They have decided that it is a waste of effort to try to convert the government, bring Christ to business, or try to influence education. So, they are trying to save souls and hang on until Christ comes again to straighten things out.

Jesus did not limit our hope to the future or our eternal destination to a heavenly place somewhere "out there." In fact, He most often talked of the Kingdom as a present reality continually increasing upon the Earth. For Jesus, it wasn't all about going to Heaven one day; it was about experiencing an increase of the Kingdom of God here on Earth, culminating in Jesus' physical reign among us at His reappearing. To Jesus, the Kingdom is a present expanding reality that will continue to advance until life on planet Earth looks just like Heaven. It is the call of the Church to make His invisible Kingdom a visible reality on Planet Earth.

Recently at our church, I asked for a show of hands concerning their understanding of the Kingdom of God. My question went something like this: "Raise your hand if, in your years of church attendance, when you heard the phrase 'the Kingdom of Heaven' or 'the Kingdom of God,' you thought the phrase was a reference to a future Kingdom that we will all enter after we die." Nearly everyone raised their hand. I think the results would be similar for most churches. Most Christians believe that the Kingdom of God is a future, heavenly place waiting for them when they die.

Jesus said, "Behold the Kingdom of Heaven is at hand," meaning that the reign of God was already present at Jesus' first coming. Then Jesus taught His disciples to pray, "...your Kingdom come, your will be done, on Earth as it is in Heaven." Jesus was teaching his disciples to think of the Kingdom, not as a future destination, but as a present earthly reality that would grow and eventually bring the values and reign of Heaven to Earth. Jesus told this parable concerning the Kingdom:

The Kingdom of Heaven is like a mustard seed, which a man took and planted in his field. Though it is the smallest of all seeds, yet when it grows, it is the largest of garden plants and becomes a tree, so that the birds come and perch in its branches.   *Matthew 13:31-32*

Jesus uses this parable to describe a Kingdom that is continually expanding until the knowledge of God's glory one day covers the Earth like the waters cover the seas (Hab 2:14). Although the fullness of the Kingdom will come at Jesus' physical return to Earth, the expansion of the Kingdom was initiated at His first coming and will increase until His return. Isaiah prophesied this truth when he said, "Of the increase of his government and peace there will be no end" (Isaiah 9:7).

The popular teaching that has prevailed in the West is that the only hope for the Church is the rapture, the second coming or both (depending on your view of eschatology) and that the present hope of an earthly Kingdom is minimal at best. I believe Jesus would disagree.

Jesus taught that the gates of hell would not prevail against the Church and that the Church would be victorious, to some degree, in bringing the reign of God to Earth before His return. There will be no need for the Church to storm the gates of hell in the life to come since the gates of hell will have already been trampled underfoot. The Church is still Jesus' plan A in establishing His Kingdom on Earth, and there is no Plan B.

Recapturing Jesus' Vision of the Church

Perhaps the Church has become increasingly sleepy concerning its calling and purpose, in large part, because it has adopted a view of the Kingdom of God that is almost exclusively future and other-worldly. The Church may have also become somewhat distracted by an excessive focus on the powers of darkness rather than the power of light.

Jesus' plan for His Church was for His followers to live courageously on the offensive against the forces of evil. He has also equipped each believer, through His Spirit, with the power to bring Heaven to Earth in their own sphere of influence. As God's Kingdom advances, the devil's tyranny will diminish. His kingdom will eventually be decisively defeated.

To suggest that miracles are not for today, or that we should not expect to live supernaturally in this life because the Bible has been completed or because the Apostles have died off, misses the point of the Kingdom entirely and renders the Church powerless in fulfilling its purpose. The problem with the Church is not that it is ill-equipped, under prepared or apostate. The problem with the Church is that it has lost a clear understanding of its mission, has surrendered its unity, and relinquished its power.

28

Encountering His Presence

When you gaze in awe, admiration, and wonder at something or someone, you begin to take on something of the character of the object of your worship.

N.T. Wright

Our oldest daughter Abby has always had a heart for God and the world. One day when we were putt-putting at Congo River Golf on our family vacation to Florida, Abby looked around and said, "One day this will be my home." I said, "You mean Florida?" She said, "No, the jungle." She was around five years old at the time. From a very young age, Abby's resolve has been to take the Gospel to unreached people groups somewhere in the jungle. Growing up as a pastor's kid, she grew up involved with the youth group and just about anything that was taking place at the church.

Like each of our girls, Abby loves Jesus and has always wanted to serve Him with her life; however, during her teenage years, she struggled with all the things that compete for the attention and affection of a teenage heart. She loved Jesus, but she also loved sports, friends, social media, clothes, all-night sleepovers, and the occasional boy (Ugghh).

Although her dreams never really changed, her focus often tended to drift more toward her many social allegiances than toward her relationship with Jesus. All of this changed as we began to experience the presence of God together as a family.

The hunger that had grown in me and Tara spread to our children, as well. There was a season when we traveled, wherever necessary, to experience the presence of God. For a solid year, we would pick one weekend per month, jump in the minivan, and travel to wherever we thought God wanted us to go. We logged a lot of miles on our minivan that year, but we had an amazing adventure together experiencing God's presence on a whole new level.

One particular weekend, we traveled several hundred miles to attend a conference. Heidi and Rolland Baker, missionaries to Mozambique, were scheduled as guest speakers at the conference. During Heidi's message, the presence of God was so strong that people wept openly throughout the auditorium.

After her message, Heidi gave an invitation for those who wanted to surrender their lives to missions. Abby responded along with many others. Up front, by the stage, Abby kneeled with her face to the ground weeping. As we kneeled at the front, Heidi made her way through the sea of people that had gathered and began praying for Abby.

Heidi whispered prayers into Abby's ear that matched prayers that Abby had been praying in her own personal time with God. Abby lay on the floor for some time afterward. She will tell you that this one encounter with God has changed her life more than all of my Sunday morning sermons; humbling but true.

A Love Deficiency

I believe my greatest struggle as a pastor can be summarized as a love deficiency. Most Christians believe in the love of God on a theological or rational level, but some, like me, had only encountered His love in small doses because we subtly believe that any experience of God is either dangerous or impossible.

If our theology about God does not lead us to an encounter of Him, we settle for religion and miss out on the intimacy He desires for us. This is not to say that we can somehow arrive at our theological conclusions through encounter alone, rather, our encounters of God must be grounded and substantiated by the Scriptural truths concerning

His immanence and character. Said another way, the written Word of God is the foundation to which our encounters with God are tethered.

I had often taught on the need for a "personal relationship" with God through Jesus, but never really paused to consider how a personal relationship requires intimacy and affection. I guess for me, a personal relationship with God was more about learning another truth about Him rather than encountering His personhood.

Sound Doctrine and Encounter

Evangelicals often stress the importance of learning sound doctrine; Charismatics typically stress the importance of encounter. The Bible emphasizes the importance of both; one cannot be separated from the other. Through truth we are introduced to the reality of God and His work in the world; through encounters of the truth, He becomes real and present in and through our lives. Sound doctrine and encounter are not mutually exclusive pursuits in the Kingdom. Rolland Baker eloquently writes:

Stories and Miracles are a critical part of the Kingdom, and so is sound doctrine. That's why Jesus taught half the time, and why God gave us the New Testament epistles. What we think about God directly affects how we feel about Him. That's my point in the Harvest School. I keep hearing that nobody gets saved by doctrine, and what we need is the Presence, not theology. All that cerebral stuff is for advanced specialists, not the outside world of lost sinners, but the first revival started when Peter got up and preached sound doctrine, and people were cut to the heart by the Holy Spirit. The presence comes through the Word   *II Timothy 3:16*

The greatest argument in support of divine encounter is Scripture. In fact, nearly every Scriptural reference to transformation is somehow connected to an encounter with God's presence. It would be difficult to read through the Psalms and somehow overlook David's obsession with God's presence. It would also be strange to imagine somehow that Moses was unchanged by his mountaintop encounters with God's glory; his glowing face would suggest otherwise.

Paul powerfully met Jesus on the road to Damascus where he heard Jesus' voice from Heaven and was struck temporarily blind. Ironically, this wasn't even his most notable encounter with God's presence. Jacob wrestled with Jesus in His pre-incarnate form and walked with a limp for the rest of his life. Enoch walked with God. Elijah was taken to Heaven in a fiery chariot.

The stories of transformation through encounter are so plentiful that it's difficult to find Scriptural examples of transformation that occurred apart from such encounters. The takeaway should be clear; we were created by God to love Him, to be loved by Him and to encounter His presence.

Moody, Finney, and Others

The most significant revivals in Church history were sparked by those who experienced God in supernatural ways. Some of the most influential leaders the Church has known found transformation, not only through knowledge of the truth but through an encounter of Him. Truth is more than information; truth is a person and it is essential that we encounter Him (John 14:6). D.L. Moody describes one experience with the Holy Spirit this way:

> *I kept on crying all the time that God would fill me with the Holy Spirit. Well, one day in the city of New York – oh! What a day, I cannot describe it. I seldom refer to it. It is almost too sacred an experience to name. Paul had an experience of which he never spoke for fourteen years. I can only say, God revealed Himself to me, and I had such an experience of His love that I had to ask Him to stay His hand.*

Charles Finney, a Presbyterian law clerk and a chief voice in the second Great Awakening describes one dramatic experience He had with the Holy Spirit:

> *The Holy Spirit descended upon me in a manner that seemed to go through me, body and soul. I could feel the impression, like a wave of electricity going through and through me. Indeed, it seemed to come in waves and waves of*

liquid love...it seemed like the very breath of God...I wept aloud with joy and love; and I do not know but I should say, I literally bellowed out the unutterable gushings of the heart. These waves came over me, and over me, and over me, one after the other, until I recollect, I cried out, "I shall die if these waves continue to pass over me." I said, "Lord, I cannot bear anymore."

Billy Graham, John and Charles Wesley, Jonathan Edwards, and others have also written about the encounters that sparked their passion and zeal for God.

During the wilderness wanderings, the Israelites came to depend upon God's presence as their sole source of direction, comfort, and safety. As they prepared to enter the Land of Promise, God asked Moses to go on ahead. However, He then informed Moses that He would not be going along with them into the land. Moses responded by saying: "If your Presence does not go with us, do not send us up from here." (Exodus 33:15)

Moses had grown to love the presence of God so much that nothing the Promised Land had to offer could compete with it. In effect, Moses was saying: "I would rather stay out here in the desert with you than to enter the promised land without you." David's longing for God's presence is evident when he cries out, "As the deer pants for streams of water, so my soul pants for you, my God" (Psalm 42:1).

There appears to be a consistent link in Scripture between regular encounters of God's presence and transformation. Some have accepted the truth of God's love on an intellectual level but have not been open to the radical transformation that comes through deeper encounters of His love. God's love can only penetrate our hearts when we encounter Him experientially. He invites us into a relational journey where we increasingly discover His goodness and love.

It has become customary to receive Jesus as Savior, securing a "golden ticket" to Heaven, yet experience very little of the abundant life Jesus promised. When our roots fail to go down deep into the soil of God's love, we lack the fruit that grows through abiding in Him. The Psalmist invites his readers to experience the goodness of God with our senses; "Taste and see that the Lord is good" (Psalm 34:8).

It's All about Love

There is no set pattern or formula which defines God's activity in our lives. We might encounter the transforming power of God's love in an infinite number of ways. An encounter with God need not include dramatic manifestations in order to be life changing. Also, God seems to care just as much about the journey as the destination. I suppose He enjoys the relational intimacy that comes with the process. Though some encounters may be especially memorable, most of the healing and freedom we experience in our lives will take place over time through repeated encounters of His love.

God's love is the goal of our encounters with Him, not the encounter itself. We are not after His gifts or blessings; we are after Him. I share this because some begin chasing after the "feeling" associated with an encounter of the Holy Spirit when all we need is a continual steady dose of His love, with or without a tangible feeling or manifestation. Regardless of how He accomplishes it, God desires to heal our deep wounds and use our greatest weaknesses to bring freedom and transformation to others. One day in the Synagogue, Jesus stood up and read from the scroll of Isaiah:

> *The Spirit of the Lord is upon me, because he has anointed me to preach the Gospel to the poor; He has sent me to heal the broken-hearted, to proclaim liberty to the captives and recovery of sight to the blind, to set at liberty those who are oppressed, and to proclaim the acceptable year of the Lord.* *Luke 4:18*

Jesus came to set us free from bondage and heal our broken hearts. He came to free all those who are "oppressed by the devil" (Acts 10:38). He came to deliver us from the prison of our sinful lifestyles and to heal our physical, emotional, and spiritual wounds. He came to establish our identity as fully loved children of God and to free us from the oppression of the devil's tyranny. We were created for deep intimate connection with the Father, apart from this connection we cannot experience the abundant life Jesus promised.

29

Tornados And Strawberry Shortcake

**The Bible assumes as a self-evident fact that men can
know God with at least the same degree of immediacy as
they know any other person or thing that comes within
the field of their experience.**

A.W. Tozer

One of the greatest gifts God has given us for Kingdom living and
the healing of our wounded hearts is imagination. Through the
imagination, God can reveal the truth that transcends the limits of our
understanding. Through the imagination, God calls us into a
supernatural journey filled with wonder, freedom and impossible
adventure.

Through the imagination, God heals our broken hearts and frees us
from the bondage that has hindered our true identity as sons and
daughters of the King. Genuine transformation in Christ is birthed in
the imagination; this is a foundational truth that is somewhat overlooked
in the Church today.

To some extent, we are all broken and wounded souls. Our identity
is largely shaped by the perceived reality that is often attached to
memories. When I was around five, my parents rushed me and my
siblings to the basement because a tornado had been spotted in our area.
I had just eaten strawberry shortcake and, due to the anxiety of the

moment, it didn't stay down long.

For years, I couldn't eat strawberry shortcake without getting an upset stomach. Even the thought of it would make me queasy. Somehow my mind connected the feelings of fear and anxiety associated with the tornado to strawberry shortcake. Whenever I tried to eat this dessert, in the years that followed, something was triggered in me that caused me to feel sick.

Many of the past events that trap our souls and hinder our lives are much more difficult and traumatic than my near tornado experience. From the rape victim who struggles with feelings of worthlessness even though she is greatly desired and loved by her husband, to the orphan who feels unwanted and lonely though he has been adopted and accepted into a loving family.

The imagination, created by God for good, becomes a theater of memories playing back, often in vivid detail, the traumatic event or events that we long to forget. Our past sins, or the sins of others committed against us, play over and over in our memories. That which God created to bless and empower us, becomes an avenue for the devil to kill, steal and destroy.

The devil will often use memories of failure or abuse to bring feelings of condemnation or hopelessness. He is the father of lies. If we are not aware of his tactics, we will begin to believe the lies he whispers to us. Though we long for freedom, we are constantly hampered by feelings, often connected to old wounds, which are brought to the surface by the most unlikely of triggers – a smell, a song, a phrase, a color, an emotion – even strawberry shortcake.

To the rational mind, our bondage may seem illogical and unreasonable; we are, nevertheless, hampered by the perceived reality that our damaged self has created with assistance from the enemy. Often, we are unaware that our dysfunctional behavior has any connection to our past wounds; some of these wounds we may not even consciously remember.

Some of us are in bondage to the lies the devil has fostered through years of causing us to view ourselves through the eyes of our failures and wounds. Though we are sought after by others, we have difficulty believing that anyone could actually value, love or desire us – even God.

Though we long to be loved, we sabotage most relationships because we can only see ourselves through the broken image the devil has created for us. Though others affirm us, we continue to believe that we are stupid, unattractive, boring, unlovable and worthless. Into this false reality, the living person of Jesus must enter. Through the imagination, God enables us to rediscover our true worth as His sons and daughters. Jesus comes and reestablishes our identity through the use of our sanctified imagination. Richard Foster writes:

> *You can actually encounter the living Christ…be addressed by His voice and be touched by His healing power. It can be more than an exercise of the imagination; it can be a genuine confrontation. Jesus Christ will actually come to you.*

As we quiet our hearts and set our affection upon Him, He will meet us in this place and reveal His love. As you focus your mind and heart upon Him, ask Him to take you on a journey, wherever He wishes. Go with Him where He leads and give Him the freedom to take you into the wounds and brokenness of your past.

Begin to trust the images and scenes that flash before your mind. He is showing you reality, not fantasy. Ask Him questions and wait for His response. The devil will try to hinder this process because it is the freedom of God's children and the power unleashed through our healed identity that the devil fears most. Make this an ongoing practice as you meet with God in the secret place.

My Personal Journey into Freedom

At one point in our journey, when we were discovering God's heart to heal our wounds, Tara and I were having a rather intimate conversation when God directed the conversation to me. As we talked, the Holy Spirit led her to ask questions that penetrated the deepest part of my heart. It was as if God himself were asking these penetrating questions through her. Over the next couple of hours, the Holy Spirit, through Tara, took me to memories I had forgotten or had repressed from years past. God began to bring into my mind feelings of loss and pain that were connected to events of my distant past.

God used my mind (imagination) to remind me of events from my past that had affected my identity and brought dysfunction into my life. Deep healing began to occur as I discovered God's love and care for me. My heart was set free when I felt God's compassion for wounds I had pressed down and neglected for years. Along with buckets of tears, I felt God's immense compassion and love for me. God, through my imagination, went to the broken little boy that still resides inside of me and brought healing through His love.

Over the next few months, God continued peeling away the calloused layers of my heart like an onion. Jesus, the great physician, performs surgery on our broken hearts and brings healing to wounds we have carried for years. I believe through encounters like these, Jesus fulfills His mission to free captives, release prisoners and heal broken hearts. Paul describes this process in his prayer for the Ephesians:

And I pray that you, being rooted and established in love, may have power, together with all the Lord's holy people, to grasp how wide and long and high and deep is the love of Christ, and to know this love that surpasses knowledge— that you may be filled to the measure of all the fullness of God. Eph 3:17-19

Notice, Paul describes the process of transformation as an intimate interaction with the love of God. Paul's prayer is for the Ephesians to "know this love that surpasses knowledge." The Greek word *gnosis*, unlike our English word, suggests a knowledge that transcends informational awareness. It includes experiential knowledge, experience or encounter.

Paul is praying that the Ephesians will experience the love of God in ways that exceed head knowledge. He believes transformation will occur for the Ephesians when they are filled with the "fullness of God" through an intense encounter of His incomprehensible love. When we encounter Jesus in our imagination, we are not encountering a fantasy of Him; we are encountering the real Jesus.

My theological background did not leave much room for an

experience of Jesus in this manner. Although theologically, I was aware that the Holy Spirit was a person, I had not been interacting with Him as such. Persons are to be experienced and encountered, not just studied for theological reasons. Though I would speak of the Holy Spirit as a person, I often related to him as an impersonal force or a theological truth. Again, Gordon Fee adds insight:

> *Life in the present is empowered by the God who dwells among us and in us. As the personal presence of God, the Spirit is not merely some "force" or "influence." The living God is a God of power, and by the Spirit, the power of the living God is present with and for us.*

When we meet the Holy Spirit as a person, He frees us from the bondage of the enemy and establishes our true identity as sons and daughters through intense encounters of His love.

A Lesson from My Daughters

One day, God gently asked me a question (not audibly) about my relationship with my daughters. It went something like this, "Chuck, would you settle for a strictly intellectual relationship with your daughters? Would you be satisfied with knowing everything about them (their height, hair color, talents, dreams, etc.), while never being able to experience their love? No hugs, no butterfly kisses, no affection, no intimate interaction?"

My emotional response was, "No, God, I would not be satisfied with that." I already knew where He was going with this. My heart came alive when my spirit heard him say, "Then, why do you think I would want anything less from you, my son?" At that moment I realized that for years I had kept God at a theological distance because I was afraid to experience Him.

Ironically, it has been through the experience of God's presence that I have been able to make sense of many Scriptures concerning the transformative power of His love. I have come to believe it is impossible to fully know God without experiencing Him as a person. Just as in Jesus, a human face was put on God the Father, so also in Jesus, a human face was put on the Holy Spirit. He is a person, not a thing, not a force. When we encounter Him, we encounter the living personhood of God; this is why Jesus prayed for the disciples by saying:

Now, this is eternal life: that they may know you, the only true God, and Jesus Christ, whom you have sent.   *John 17:3*

For much of my Christian life, including most of my life as a pastor, I have been somewhat closed off to encounters of the Lord's presence. Maybe "closed off" is not the best terminology. I suppose a better description would be that I was somewhat afraid or felt unworthy to encounter or experience God in tangible ways.

To be honest, for many years, I was fully content with my academic pursuits of God and a more formal approach to His presence. I knew it was my responsibility to follow, serve, and obey Him, but I had no idea He wanted much more from me; things like love, romance, and intimacy. Sadly, despite years of ministry, I was unaware that God was so much fun! I had no idea His presence is full of such joy and that He has wonderful adventures planned for us to experience together.

Maybe, for whatever reason, you have lived your Christian life like me, closed off to supernatural encounters with God. Maybe today that could all change. You can begin right now by placing all of your affection upon Him and asking Him to meet with you. Take time right now and ask God this question: "What do you think of me?" Wait for His answer and trust the words you hear or the pictures you see as genuine. Allow Him to take you to a secret place set aside for just you and Him. Talk to Him, listen for His voice and open up your heart to His love. God will use your imagination to speak to you as His son or daughter. You were designed to hear from Him and encounter Him in this way.

Tell Him you love Him and long to experience His goodness, however He may choose. God is absolutely crazy about you, but He will not force His love upon you. He longs to heal the brokenness in your heart, but He will not barge in uninvited to do so. After all, forced love is not really love at all. He longs to be with you. He longs for your company. He loves to listen to your dreams and calm all your fears.

When you give yourself fully to Him, He will give Himself fully to you. It's the reason you're alive; it's the reason you were created. You were made for Him. You were made for love. You were made for the presence of the living God.

Sleepy Christians

30

Your Journey Begins Here

**Don't worry that you're not strong enough
before you begin. It is in the Journey
that God makes you strong.**

Anonymous

I absolutely love fishing for walleye. I caught the bug as a teenager fishing in Canada with a group of guys every summer. Living with five girls, you might imagine my days of wilderness camping have vanished and have been replaced with week-long trips to outlet malls and beauty salons, but not so. Most summers our family packs up the minivan and heads north to Quebec for our annual wilderness walleye fishing trip, and my girls love it. It's crazy-beautiful up there with little to no distraction from the civilized world.

A few years ago, I was fishing with the girls at one of our favorite fishing spots on our favorite lake in Quebec, and we were absolutely "slaying" the walleye. I was fishing in one boat with Emma and Josie while Tara was in another boat with Abby and Ellie. The sun was going down, and since we had been fishing a few miles from camp, the girls were ready to head back to our island. I, on the other hand, have a difficult time calling it quits while the fish are still biting. After all, what if my next fish is the monster. I've been waiting for all my life?

By the time I finally agreed to head in, it had gotten rather dark on the lake. We started our motors, took a quick look at the trees for directional purposes, and took off at full speed toward the cabin, or so we thought. It was Tara who first recognized that we were going in the wrong direction. By the time she was able to get my attention, we had traveled for ten to fifteen minutes at full speed in the wrong direction. To make matters worse, there are rocks just below the surface of the water in this lake, and we had been heading directly for a whole mess of them.

As we sat in our boats, miles from camp in complete darkness, I began to grow somewhat concerned. I tried not to sound alarmed for the girl's sake, but Tara and I both knew the reality of our situation. We were lost! I had a feeling each of us were talking to God about the bleakness of our circumstances as we headed off, very slowly, toward what we hoped was the direction of our island. It was so dark by this point we couldn't be completely sure we were traveling in the right direction. The tall pine trees on the hills were just dark shadows lining the perimeter of the lake in every direction.

As we putted along, staying far enough from shore to avoid hidden rocks, I imagined what it would be like sleeping in our boats in the open water until morning. I somewhat regretted my attempt to "freak out" the girls with talks of the large number of bears and wolves that lived close to our island. After what seemed like an eternity, we rounded a corner and saw a faint light in the distance. It was our island. We all let out a yell, and then I said, "I knew where we were the whole time." Everyone laughed! Since that night, I have been less reluctant to wait for the fish to stop biting before heading back to camp.

Beginning Your Supernatural Journey

I believe each one of us has been invited to go on an amazing, supernatural Journey with God. Some of us are going full speed ahead but haven't stopped to consider if we are traveling in a direction that will lead us to our supernatural destination. A life of freedom and adventure lies just beyond the boundaries of our religious and intellectual mindsets. The supernatural journey will require us to stop, recapture our bearings and follow the Holy Spirit into the "more" of God. There is more to this journey than just going fast. You also need to be going in the right direction.

God has given each of us a personal invitation and longs for us to join Him in living the way we were created to live fully free and fully alive. My prayer is that somewhere in the course of reading this book you have dealt with the mental and theological blocks that have held you back from experiencing the abundant life God has planned for you. If you are still in the process, that's okay, so am I and so is everyone on the planet, whether they know it or not. After all, God is inviting us to come along with Him on a "journey." A journey usually implies that there is a process involved.

Positioning for Encounter

Though great walleye fishing is never a guarantee, we have discovered if we follow some of the lessons we have learned over the years, we are likely to catch the big ones sooner or later. We have learned the feeding habits of walleye, the places where they prefer to hang out, and the best techniques to catch them—so our chances are usually pretty good we will end up with a stringer full of walleye by the end of the day. We can't make the walleye bite, but we can position ourselves in ways that give us the greatest opportunity to catch them.

We have learned that walleye love rocky bottoms and somewhat cooler waters. We have also discovered they feed more often when the light levels are low or when there is a bit of a chop on the water. Types and colors of lures also change with the season, water temperature and the availability of baitfish. Fishing in the right place at the right time with the appropriate lure will give us the best opportunity to catch walleye. Though we already have God's grace (favor) freely available to us, positioning ourselves to receive from Him is still important. Creating "space" in our lives for God to show up is essential to encountering more of Him.

Creating Space for God to Fill

Creating space to be with God alone in the secret place is essential to the supernatural journey. The greatest enemy to our intimacy with

God is often our own schedules. I have heard it said that busyness is the business of the devil and I would agree. We do not earn God's presence, but it's also true that we can't encounter someone we don't make time for. Calvin Miller comments on this by saying:

> *One who wants an in-depth affair with Christ must not allow time clocks and ledger sheets to destroy that wonderful holy leisure by which we make friends with God. To be a godly disciple means that we transcend the clock; because to be with God mandates that we give our life to become one who waits on God for the sheer pleasure of His company.*

I'm a huge football fan. It's a rare occasion when I fail to make time in my schedule to watch my favorite team play football. Somehow, I always seem to be available for the three hours necessary to watch the game. Why is it that we find it easy to say no to competing agendas for the sake of something as fleeting as a sporting event yet have difficulty saying no for the sake of our time alone with God? We might easily say, "I'm sorry, I have that time scheduled for God," or simply, "I have a prior arrangement scheduled at that time." Consistently honoring our time alone with God will produce transformation in our lives and great fruit for the Kingdom. Finding space in our schedules for God will not happen accidently.

We must be proactive in guarding our schedules and prioritizing our time alone with Him. I am amazed that whenever I clean out my garage, creating extra free space, it takes very little time for those spaces to become cluttered once again. Like my garage, the empty spaces in our lives tend to fill up rather quickly with the busyness and lure of other urgent matters. Being intentional with our calendars and prioritizing His presence will go a long way toward ensuring consistent time alone with Him. The power of routine can work for or against us here, depending on how we routinely spend our time. John Michael Talbot writes:

> *By practicing the discipline of solitude, we are creating space in our lives where God can be with us. And over time, as that space grows, so can our relationship with the living God.*

Nothing attracts God's presence like worship. I am not merely referring to our expressions of praise offered through singing songs, though this can certainly play a part. More specifically, I am talking about placing all of our adoration and affection upon Him regardless of the time or location. There's something about the focused affection of our hearts that connects us to Him like little else.

What better way to interact with someone than to set aside regular time to be alone with them? As a dad, setting aside time to "date" my daughters has been key to the closeness we share. Though God is always available and willing to meet with us at any time, our hearts are better prepared to receive from Him when we are free from distraction.

Jesus consistently made space in His life to be alone with the Father. He routinely escaped the pressures of the crowds to find a quiet place to be still and listen for his Father's voice. Mark writes, "Very early in the morning, while it was still dark, Jesus got up, left the house and went off to a solitary place, where he prayed." (Mark 1:35)

This was Jesus' pattern repeated throughout the Gospels. I have found it difficult to encounter God without creating space in my schedule to meet with Him regularly. If this concept is new for you, don't get discouraged if your time with God is sporadic or if you have to start small. God is not judging your commitment level. I believe that He is thrilled with any effort you put forth, regardless of how insignificant you think it to be. As your desire grows, you will begin to find time where you thought there was none and your hunger for His presence will continue to grow.

It is equally important that we make space within our schedules to encounter God together with others in community. When we encounter God alone and then carry His presence with us into community, the Kingdom of God manifests mightily within our gatherings. We can then go, with a heart filled with God's love, into a desperate world and bring Heaven to Earth. Prioritizing God's presence alone and in community is vital to the supernatural journey.

Where's Your Secret Place?

The ideal secret place will be different for everyone. My wife loves to spend time with God in the beauty of nature where she can appreciate His handiwork. Although I love God's creation, I need to be in a place where there are absolutely no distractions (squirrel!) like in a dark, quiet room with a single candle. Regardless, your time alone with Him should focus on one thing – drawing near to Him. Henri Nouwen eloquently writes:

> *Without solitude, it is virtually impossible to live a spiritual life. Solitude begins with a time and place for God, and him alone. If we believe not only that God exists but also that He is actively present in our lives – healing, teaching and guiding – we need to set aside a time and space to give Him our undivided attention. Jesus says, "Go to your private room and, when you have shut the door, pray to your Father who is in the secret place."*

Consistent time alone with God will eventually lead us to the realization that He is with us. His presence becomes our conscious reality throughout the mundane moments of our daily lives. We discover, like the Psalm writer, that when we dwell in the secret place with the most-high God, His presence overshadows us everywhere we go (Psalm 91:1). Regardless of where our daily adventures take us, we discover that we actually never leave His abiding presence.

When You Fast

The idea of fasting may be new to you; I was a pastor for over 20 years before I ever taught on the principle of fasting. However, Jesus assumed that fasting would be a consistent part of our walk with God. Jesus taught fasting as a way of bringing the desires of our fleshly nature in line with His Spirit. Jesus did not say "If you fast," He said, "When you fast," indicating that fasting should be a regular part of the normal Christian life.

We don't fast for God; We don't fast to earn His favor or to get Him to do something for us. His love and favor toward us are unaffected by our fasting. We fast to increase our hunger for spiritual things and to train our nature to submit to God. Fasting is one way for our spirit to show our human nature that it doesn't call the shots. The body is a good servant but a horrible master; fasting is a way to bring our bodies into submission to our spirits. As Paul put it, "I buffet my body…" Fasting is the power behind our willpower, it is the atomic bomb for our spiritual life.

Once again, I am not implying that disciplined behaviors, like fasting and prayer, are the primary starting points for transformation. Transformation always begins with an encounter of the Father's love. However, when we encounter His love in radical ways, we are given the fuel (desire) to pursue Him. Once He captures our affection, we will do for love with very little effort what we could never do through discipline alone. We do not fast and pray so we can earn His favor, we fast because we already have His favor and we long for even greater intimacy with Him.

Stressed Out Pastors

In recent years, I have had the opportunity to share our story with many pastors and church leaders. I have been struck with the great weight many of them are carrying. I think it's fair to say, many church leaders are overwhelmed with their ministries and have little joy evident in their lives. I find it easy to relate to them since I have felt the same burden at times in ministry.

There are tremendous demands placed on pastors, spoken and unspoken, to grow and educate the church. Many pastors are forced to wear multiple hats – leader, preacher, teacher, counselor, CEO, janitor, maintenance worker, etc. I love to meet with pastors and leaders who are at the "end of their rope" because I can feel their pain. I long for them to find the freedom and peace which comes from Supernatural Rest. My heart hurts for them because I have walked many years in their shoes.

Though it may surprise you, I have found that pastors, like other followers of Jesus, often struggle to encounter God's manifest presence; this may seem odd on the surface, but it makes sense when you stop and think about it. Sometimes, as pastors, we become so busy serving God that we fail to take opportunities to sit at His feet and soak in His glory. Like Martha, we load up our schedules with many tasks when only one thing is needful – His presence.

Also, pastors often feel like they are on an island with no one to talk to. We spend much of our time teaching, counseling and leading, but rarely have the luxury of receiving ministry from others. We often feel overwhelmed, burned out and incapable of leading people. There is no course offered in most Bible schools or seminaries on the topic of resting in God's presence.

More often than not, prayer becomes another task listed on our job description, just another thing to do. Simply put, for many pastors, encountering God's presence is not much on our radar. It sounds like more work and added stress, just another task on our to-do list; this was a reality in my life and ministry, though I was somewhat blind to it for many years.

It's crazy, I knew how to preach a sermon, teach a class, run a meeting, and lead a team, but I didn't know how to experience the manifest presence of God. As a result, I consumed far less grace in His presence than was available to me. I often tried to minister in my own strength apart from His power. I was working for Him rather than from Him. There were somewhat artificial results and plenty of burnout.

Ironically, we pastors have been trained well to do the business of church, but we haven't been adequately trained to do the one thing that matters most, encounter the presence of the living God. Many of us work tirelessly for Him, relentlessly hoping to gain His approval. We imagine the day we will see Him face to face and hear Him say, "Well done good and faithful servant." In contrast to tirelessly working, Heidi Baker has commented:

If pastors would just lie down on the floor and act like a bunch of dead people, they would get something done in the church.

As pastors, if we can learn the neglected truth of supernatural rest, we can let go of our striving and begin seeing supernatural fruit for God's Kingdom in our lives and ministries. Unfortunately, rest is not something that most pastors do well, at least without feeling guilty.

31

Aslan Is On The Move

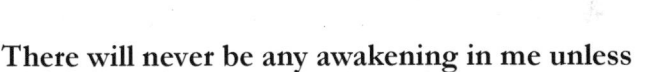

**There will never be any awakening in me unless
I am called out of darkness by Him who is light.**
Thomas Merton

The absolute best time to be out in the boat walleye fishing in Quebec is in the early morning just as the sun is coming up. The water is often super calm with a foggy mist coming off of it. The loons, who always seem to wake first, celebrate the dawn of the new day with relentless calls of laughter. If I didn't know better, I would swear they were laughing at me. The morning is bliss; what joy comes with each awakening.

I remember one, early, summer morning fishing adventure many years ago on a beautiful Canadian lake. I was with my friend, Brian, headed through a misty fog toward a newly discovered fishing spot when we saw what appeared to be a pirate ship ahead in the distance. As we continued through the fog, closer to the pirate ship, we began to see reality a bit clearer.

What looked very much like a pirate ship, from a foggy distance, was just an island with tall pines that looked much like the sails of a pirate ship. A combination of the fog and the grogginess of the morning had distorted the reality of what we were actually seeing. For a brief moment, it looked like we were gonna have a throw down with a group of rowdy pirates over our new fishing spot. Thankfully, it never had to come to that!

Wake Up! You Might Miss Something

On the night Jesus was betrayed and handed over to be crucified, He was in the Garden of Gethsemane with the disciples. Throughout the night, Jesus asked them to stay awake and pray while He went off to be with the Father. Every time Jesus returned from prayer, He found the disciples asleep. Jesus said to them: "Couldn't you men keep watch with me for one hour" (Matthew 26:40)? Like the disciples, if we don't wake up, we might miss something extremely significant. The Kingdom of God is on the move, but we can easily miss it in our slumber.

God is pouring out His Spirit today like never before. Around the world, Jesus' followers are being increasingly awakened to His present Kingdom activity on Earth. The Church has not been left alone to fend for itself. Jesus is moving among His people, awakening them to the fullness of His present Kingdom. It's like Jesus is saying, "Come on, wake up, you don't want to miss this." Isaiah 60 is a prophetic picture of God's activity in the Church in our day. The Prophet Isaiah writes:

> *Arise, shine, for your light has come,*
> *and the glory of the Lord rises upon you.*
> *See, darkness covers the Earth*
> *and thick darkness is over the peoples,*
> *but the Lord rises upon you*
> *and his glory appears over you.*
> *Nations will come to your light,*
> *and kings to the brightness of your dawn.*
>
> *Isaiah 60:1-3*

Is it possible that God is calling the Church to wake up? It's not that we are sound asleep, but we are not fully awakened to His plan and intent for the Church. We, like the disciples, are in danger of napping through the greatest move of God planet Earth has ever witnessed. It's time for God's people to wake up to supernatural transformation, abundant living and the overpowering, all-consuming love of God. For many of us, logic has hindered the childlike faith and expectancy that we are supposed to have as God's children. We have become limited by logic and have lost our ability to dream like children. It's time to dream again...

Awakened to Word and Spirit

Sleepy Christianity will be insufficient to bring Heaven to Earth or to destroy the works of the devil. The Kingdom will not go forward as a result of our eloquent sermons or reasoned arguments alone. There is more to the Kingdom of God than serving, teaching and witnessing in our own strength. Jesus is seeking Kingdom fighters who know both the power of the Word and the power of the Spirit. God is awakening us to the fullness of His Kingdom and its transforming power.

God longs for us to return to the childlike trust and wonder that marked our early years when we believed in the impossible and expected the extraordinary. Our supernatural God is inviting us to join Him in advancing His Kingdom like wide-eyed little children. There are dragons to be defeated and fair maidens to be rescued. We have dark kingdoms to invade and gates of hell to trample upon. It's time to fly higher, run faster, and jump farther than ever before. All of creation eagerly waits for the "revealing of the children of God" (Romans 8:19).

Awakened to the Kingdom

Though the fullness of this revealing will come when Jesus reappears, He has already set this transformative process into motion. We are no longer orphans, but children of a good Father who has granted us access to everything that belongs to Him. "His divine power has given us everything we need for life and godliness...." (II Peter 1:3). Many of us are still living like rational adults, while Jesus is calling us to live like wide-eyed, fantasy-filled children once again.

Impossibility awaits us; adventure lies just around the corner. The Kingdom of Heaven is at hand, but we are quite often too sleepy to see it or grab ahold of it. "Wake up O sleeper," your supernatural adventure awaits. Through His Spirit, we conquer Kingdoms, vanquish darkness and bring orphaned children home to the safety and bliss of their Father's house. The supernatural life lies just beyond the boundaries of our logic, fear, and offense. God is more active, more present and more fun than our sleepy condition is accustomed to recognizing.

Aslan is on the Move

C.S. Lewis does a masterful job of describing the nature of the Kingdom in his book, "The Lion, The Witch, and The Wardrobe." My favorite scene is toward the end of the book when it becomes apparent that Aslan (Jesus) is on the move. Narnia has been entrenched in continual winter due to a curse cast by the White Witch. In this scene, the children begin to see signs that Aslan is near and is restoring all things. As they walk along, they are awakened to His presence by displays of His power all around them. The snow is melting, the trees are budding, and flowers are popping up through the ground. The warmth and signs of spring are evidence that Aslan, the King of Kings, is on the move.

The children, and all of Narnia are filled with joy when they realize that the curse has been broken and the reign of the White Witch is coming to a soon and certain end. Becoming more aware of their true identity as "sons of Adam" and "daughters of Eve," the children discover that they each have a part to play in the battle against the White Witch. Aslan has invited them to partner with Him in bringing His Kingdom back to Narnia. The scene ends with the children joining Aslan in overthrowing the White Witch, as Aslan himself delivers the final and fatal blow.

Though it has gone somewhat unnoticed to much of the Church, God has been moving around the world among people groups that have been closed off to the Gospel for centuries. These places have remained in darkness until recent days. Millions have come to Christ in China as the power of God moves in the "Underground" Church through miracles, signs, and wonders. In the last decade alone, millions have turned to Jesus in Africa, where many have been raised from the dead through the prayers of childlike followers of Jesus.

Similar awakenings are taking place in Indonesia, South Korea,

South America, etc. Muslims are coming to Jesus like never before in the Middle East as Jesus appears to them in visions and dreams. Unlike any other time in Church history, God is pouring out His Spirit upon all flesh. Signs of His presence are everywhere, and many are awakening to the nearness of His Kingdom. We are living in the midst of the greatest awakening the world has ever known. It has become increasingly difficult to overlook or deny that Aslan (Jesus) is on the move.

Though the scope of God's redemptive plan is immense, reaching to the ends of creation, it is also overtly personal. If you were the only person in need of redemption, He would still have sent Jesus to pay for your sins and to prove His immense love for you. In the midst of this worldwide move of God, He desires to focus His attention on you. You are the object of His affection, the target of His love, the desire of His heart. He has a plan for you. You are His prized creation. He created you for love, and He will not withhold His pursuit of you until His love has fully awakened you to more of Him. His love is like "a blazing fire" and "a mighty flame." "Many waters cannot quench" His relentless love pursuit of you (Song of Solomon 8:6-7). Nothing can separate you from this love (Romans 8:38-39).

Many have used the term "awakening" to describe the process of transformation I have attempted to describe in this book. It's not that we have been indifferent or resistant to the Kingdom's existence; it's just that we have not been fully awakened to the Kingdom's present reality. For many of us, it's as if we are seeing the Kingdom of God in part, but our vision is foggy, and we aren't fully aware of its present reality all around us. Everything has changed now! It's not that God is more present among us now than He was before; it's just that we are becoming more aware of Him and what He is up to on planet Earth.

Awakened to Hope

Awakening fills us with hope and anticipation for all that our loving Heavenly Father desires to accomplish in and through us. When we are awakened to the fullness of His love, the skies are brighter, the air is sweeter, and each day is filled with anticipation for the impossible. We become expectant in our hope for the Church and for those who are deeply entangled in bondage to the devil. Our hearts are overwhelmed by the love and acceptance of God, and we no longer find our identity in the applause or approval of others.

As a pastor, I have fewer answers, fewer strategies, and a greater awareness of my dependence upon my Heavenly Father. I feel completely inadequate and unprepared for the assignment and call on my life, and I totally love it. When people ask me what our strategy or plan is for the future of Journey, I have no problem saying: "I don't know, but I can't wait to find out." I have come to accept that it's not my job to build the Church since Jesus said He would handle that himself (Matt 16:18). It has been amazing to watch God bring freedom and transformation apart from my one, three, or five-year plan. I am filled with more love for people and more joy for ministering to them.

I hope our story has awakened something within you. If you are overwhelmed with worry, anxiety or fear, Jesus doesn't want you there. He invites you to come and find rest in His presence. If you have lost hope or joy, God longs to fill you with supernatural hope and overflowing joy. The answer to your problems can't be found in a better plan, more money, a better job, or more vacation time. Your contentment is not dependent upon the faithfulness or performance of those around you. The answer to your brokenness and pain is unrelated to your circumstances or life situation. The answer, to everything really, is more of Him.

Many of us need to hear Jesus saying: "Enough is enough. You can't earn My favor – you already have it." Those who lead: It's time to stop being good CEO's and start being good sons and daughters. He is not impressed with our stressed-out schedules or strategic plans to change the world. He is not moved by what you do; He is moved by you. You are not responsible for building His church, that's His job. You are invited to surrender and rest in Him, only then can we bear real fruit.

Now, Go Change the World

The supernatural Journey was never intended to be a solo journey, but a journey of sharing the love and transforming power of Jesus with the world. Jesus came with a mission to serve others and love them into the Kingdom. In essence, we are all called to be freedom fighters, releasing people from the tyranny and bondage of the devil. The freedom and transformation we receive from Jesus can become the freedom and transformation available to those we encounter each day.

One day a young student of Mother Teresa asked her, "How can I be like you?" Mother Teresa answered, "Find your own Calcutta." This is the call of Jesus to each person who has encountered His transforming love; Go change the world. Jesus said, "The Son of man did not come to be served, but to serve, and to give His life as a ransom for many" (Matthew 20:28).

The joy that we encounter in God's presence multiplies when we give it away in service to others. When Jesus said, "It is more blessed to give than to receive," He was not just trying to trick us into serving; He genuinely believed that our lives would overflow with joy more through service than through being served, more through giving than receiving. The joy of our awakening is not limited to seeing and experiencing God in new and powerful ways; it is also the joy of watching those around us discover more of Him as well.

My Prayer For You

Dear God, I pray for the person reading this book right now. I pray that their heart would be awakened to your all-consuming love and compassion. I pray that their longing for you would explode as they ask for "more of you at any cost." I pray that they will learn to dream and believe like a child again and that they will begin to expect unbelievable, irrational, impossible things from you every day. I pray that you will overcome them with your love and joy and that they will encounter you in deeper ways. I pray that you will fill them with greater love for the Church, greater expectancy for your Kingdom, and an abundance of hope for their family.

God, we know that you are up to something big in this world, and that you have not left this son or daughter to watch from a distance. I pray that you fill them with unrealistic, supernatural optimism concerning their future and the future of those they love. I pray that they will begin to live with a continual conscious awareness of your power and presence, and that they would discover the great plans that you have for their life. I pray that they will surrender their heart and affection to you daily and will actively wait for you to come meet with them. I pray that they will have an incredible, supernatural journey with you, God, every day, for the rest of their life. Amen!

Notes

CHAPTER 2

Greg Boyd, Seeing is Believing (Grand Rapids, MI: Baker Books, 2004) 18

Dallas Willard, The Divine Conspiracy (San Francisco, CA: Harper Collins Publishers, 1998) 49

CHAPTER 4

David Kinnaman, Unchristian (Grand Rapides, MI: Baker Books, 2007) 80

I am not here implying that the only reason for the "back door" problem in churches is a lack of transformation. I realize that many factors are involved when an individual decides to depart for another church home. However, for our church and many like it, a lack of transformation and true family culture were major reasons people decided to "move on".

CHAPTER 5

A.W. Tozer, The Pursuit of God (Camp Hill, PA: Christian Publications Inc, 1982) 9

CHAPTER 6

David Watson, I Believe in the Church (London, England: Hodder & Stoughton, 1985)

Henry T. Blackaby and Claude V. King, Experiencing God (Nashville, TN: Broadman and Holman Publishers, 1994) 5

Bill Johnson, Face To Face With God (Lake Mary, FL: Charisma House Publishers, 2007) 8

CHAPTER 7

A.W. Tozer, The Pursuit of God (Camp Hill, PA: Christian Publications Inc, 1982) 10

Bill Johnson, Face To Face With God (Lake Mary, FL: Charisma House Publishers, 2007) 12
John Eldredge, The Sacred Romance (Nashville, TN: Thomas Nelson Publishers, 1997) 73

CHAPTER 8

Chuck Coulson, quoted by David Kinnaman, Unchristian (Grand Rapides, MI: Baker Books, 2007) 80

For a detailed description of the "treasure hunt" read Kevin Dedmon, The Ultimate Treasure Hunt (Shippensburg, PA: Destiny Image Publishers, 2007)

CHAPTER 12

Dallas Willard, The Divine Conspiracy (San Francisco, CA: Harper Collins Publishers, 1998) 50

CHAPTER 13

Gordon Fee, God's Empowering Presence (Peabody, MA: Hendrickson Publishers, 1994) 9

CHAPTER 15

Jack Deere, Surprised By The Power of The Spirit (Grand Rapids, MI: Zondervan Publishing House, 1995)

Relegating the miraculous to an elite few gifted individuals is possibly the greatest lesson than we can learn from the "failings" of the healing ministries of the past century. It was widely held that the ministry of healing was reserved for a few specially gifted individuals rather than the entire body of believers.

Notes

CHAPTER 16

Francis MacNutt, The Practice of Healing Prayer (Frederick, MD: The Word Among Us Press, 2010) 23

Dallas Willard, The Spirit of the Disciplines (San Francisco, CA: Harper and Row Publishers, 1988) 54

CHAPTER 18

For a good scholarly book on the prophetic ministry today read: Jack Deere, Surprised By The Voice Of God (Grand Rapids, MI: Zondervan Publishing House, 1996)

A.W. Tozer, The Pursuit of God (Camp Hill, PA: Christian Publications Inc, 1982) 58

Ibid 105

CHAPTER 19

Charles Pinnock, Flame of Love: A Theology of the Holy Spirit (Downers Grove, IL: Inter Varsity Press, 2009) 140

J.D.G. Dunn, Spirit and Kingdom (Grand Rapids, MI: Erdmans Publishers, 1998) 133

CHAPTER 20

The Barna Group has done extensive research on the spiritual views of younger generations. You can read about some of their findings in the book by David Kinnaman entitled Unchristian, Baker Books

Also, check out www.unchristian.com/Qideas

David Kinnaman, Unchristian (Grand Rapides, MI: Baker Books, 2007) 24

Mike Foster quoted by David Kinnaman, Ibid 26

CHAPTER 21

Francis MacNutt, The Practice of Healing Prayer (Frederick, MD: The Word Among Us Press, 2010) 24

For more discussion concerning the current revival among Muslim nations see for example an article in Christianity Today entitled "We are Living in the Midst of the Greatest Turning of Muslims to Christ in History" June 17, 2015 by Lucinda Borkett-Jones.

Also, see the CBN Broadcast entitled "Visions of Jesus Stir Muslim Hearts"

CHAPTER 22

It has become commonplace in the American Church to label anything that is beyond our comfort or comprehension as "deception". This extreme skepticism toward experience and encounter has arisen, in large part, with the over emphasis the American Church has placed on the powers of darkness during the end-times.

CHAPTER 23

C.S. Lewis quoted by David Kinnaman, Unchristian (Grand Rapides, MI: Baker Books, 2007) 121

A strange thing has happened within American denominationalism over the past few centuries. It has become completely acceptable for members of differing denominations to be unloving toward one another for "theological" reasons. This has contributed to the overall ineffectiveness of the Church at working together in reaching the lost.

For information on the growing number of Protestant denominations see www.philvaz.com/apologetics/a106.htm

Saint John Climacus, The Ladder of Divine Ascent (Mahwah, NJ: Paulist Press, 1982) 254

For a discussion on the early Quakers see for example: John Cunningham, The Quakers: From Their Origin Until Present Times – An International History

Notes

(Edinburgh, Scotland: John Menzies & Co. Publishers, 1868) 22

John Piper, Desiring God (Sisters, OR: Multnomah Books, 1996) 35

Stephen Tomkins, John Wesley: A Biography (Grand Rapids and Cambridge: William B. Eerdmans Publishing Co., 2003) 90

Meister Eckhart quoted by Paul Murray, "Drinking in the Word: Dominicans and the New Wine of the Gospel," http://www.op.org/international/english/

CHAPTER 24

John Wesley, The Holy Spirit and Power (Alachua, Fl: Bridge Logos Foundation, 2003) 204

Ibid

Jonathan Edwards, The Personal Narrative of Jonathan Edwards (New York, NY: American Book Company, 1935) 37-38

Ibid

See www.wesleygospel.com/2011/05/28/ jonathan-edwards-rules-for-spiritual-discerment

Johnathan Edwards, The Distinguishing Marks of a Work of the Holy Spirit of God (1741)

This book was recently republished by Meadow Books (2007) using the same title.

Richard Rohr, Hope Against Darkness: Transforming Vision of Saint Francis in an Age of Anxiety (Cincinnati, OH: St Anthony Messenger Press, 2001)

CHAPTER 25

Bill Johnson, Experience The Impossible (Bloomington, MN: Chosen Press, 2014) 171

CHAPTER 26

John Sanders, The Openness of God (Downers Grove, IL: Inter Varsity Press, 1994) 80

Clark Pinnock, The Openness of God (Downers Grove, IL: Inter Varsity Press, 1994) 115-16

Bill Johnson, Experience The Impossible (Bloomington, MN: Chosen Press, 2014) 174

CHAPTER 27

The "rapture" has often been called "an American Phenomenon" since rapture theology originated in the United States and has failed to make a profound impact around the world.

Michael Maiden, Turn the World Upside Down (Shippensburg, PA: Destiny Image, 2011) 24

N.T. Wright, Surprised by Hope: Rethinking Heaven, the Resurrection, and the Mission of the Church (New York, NY: Harper Collins Publishers, 2008) 293

Michael Maiden, 37 Turn the World Upside Down (Shippensburg, PA: Destiny Image, 2011) 37

CHAPTER 28

Quoted from a Facebook post by Rolland Baker on March 11, 2017

Concerning Moody see www.wholesomewords.org/biography/biomoody4.html

Concerning Finney see Bernard A. Weisberger, They Gathered at the River (Boston, MA: Brown and Co., 1958) 92

CHAPTER 29

Richard Foster, Celebration of Discipline (New York, NY: Harper and Row Publishers, 1978)

Notes

Gordon Fee, God's Empowering Presence (Peabody, MA: Hendrickson Publishers, 1994) 8

CHAPTER 30

Meister Eckhart, was a German theologian, philosopher and mystic, born near Gotha, in the Landgraviate of Thuringia in the Roman Empire
Born: 1260, Tambach-Dietharz, Germany Died: 1328

A.W. Tozer, The Pursuit of God (Camp Hill, PA: Christian Publications Inc, 1982) 51

Jonathan Edwards – with James M. Houston, Faith Beyond Feelings: Discerning the Heart of True Spirituality (Chicago, IL: David C. Cook Publishing, 1998) 47

Calvin Miller, The Disciplined Life (Grand Rapids, MI: Baker Book House, 2011)

John M. Talbot, The Lessons of Saint Francis: How to Bring Simplicity and Spirituality into Your Daily Life

For additional discounted copies of Sleepy Christians, visit
www.sleepychristians.com

The Sleepy Christian Study Guide is designed to assist individuals or small groups in their supernatural journey with God. The Study Guide comes with a link to 10 video discussion starters, one for each lesson. Order extra copies at a discounted rate at **www.sleepychristians.com**